Tim Davis

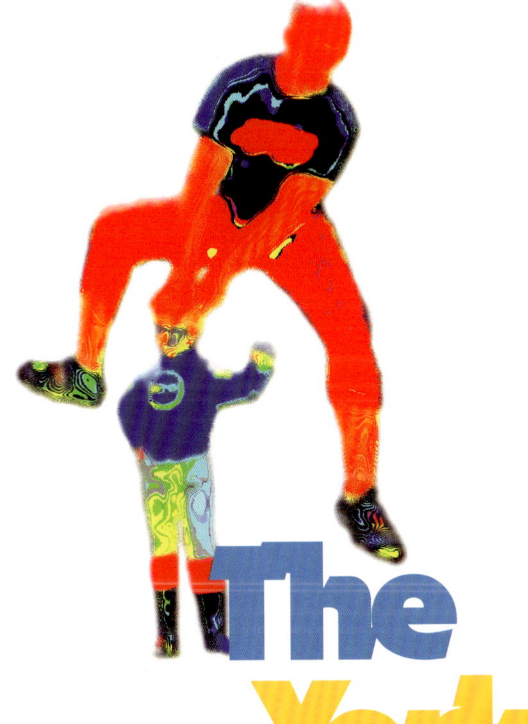

The Upstate New York Olympics

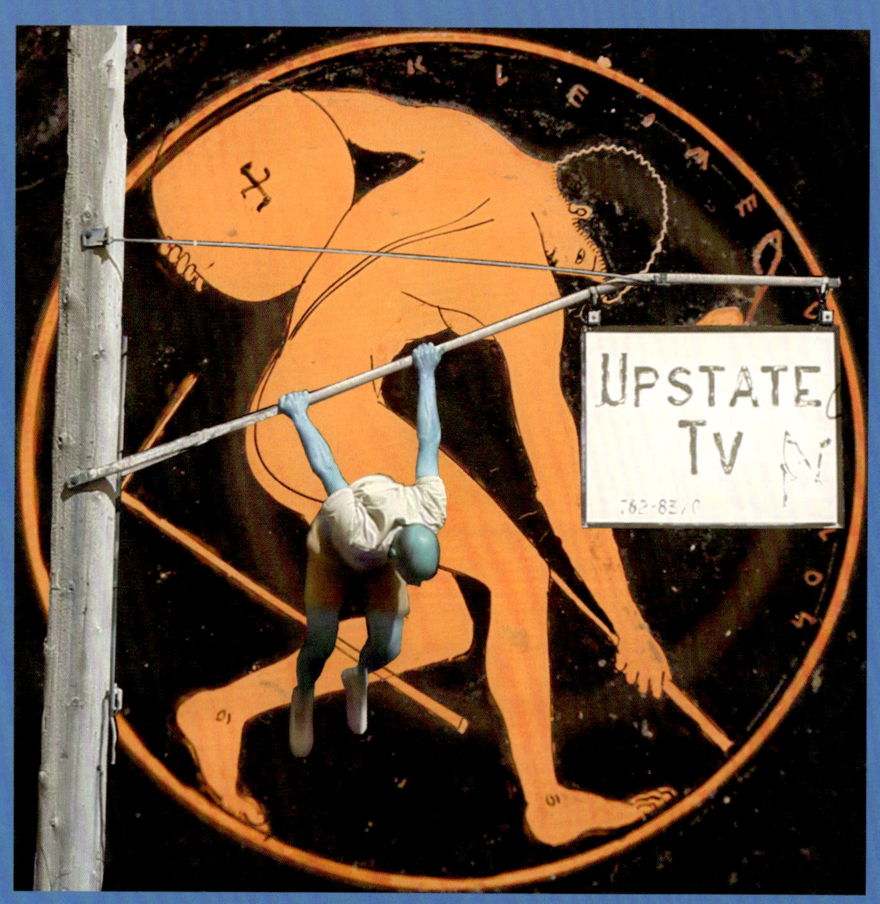

UPSTATE
TV
762-8370

Published on the occasion of the exhibition *The Upstate New York Olympics: Tim Davis*, curated by Brian Wallace, on display from March 30 through July 17, 2011, in the Howard Greenberg Family Gallery of the Samuel Dorsky Museum of Art.

This catalogue was funded by the New York Council for the Humanities. Additional support was provided by the Friends of the Samuel Dorsky Museum of Art and the Greenberg Van Doren Gallery, New York.

Published by the Samuel Dorsky Museum of Art
State University of New York at New Paltz
One Hawk Drive
New Paltz, New York 12561

Designed by the Office of Communication & Marketing: Design Services, State University of New York at New Paltz.

Distributed by the State University of New York Press (www.sunypress.edu).

ISBN No. 978-0-615-40182-9

Printed by Lithography by Design, Highland, NY, using vegetable-based inks on Chorus Art, an acid and elemental chlorine-free paper containing a minimum of 30 percent post-consumer recovered fiber.

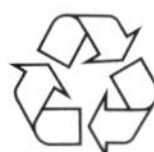
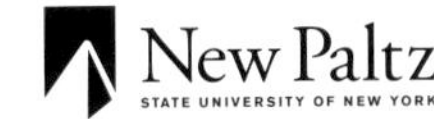

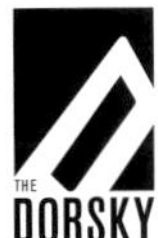

New York Council for the Humanities

Contents

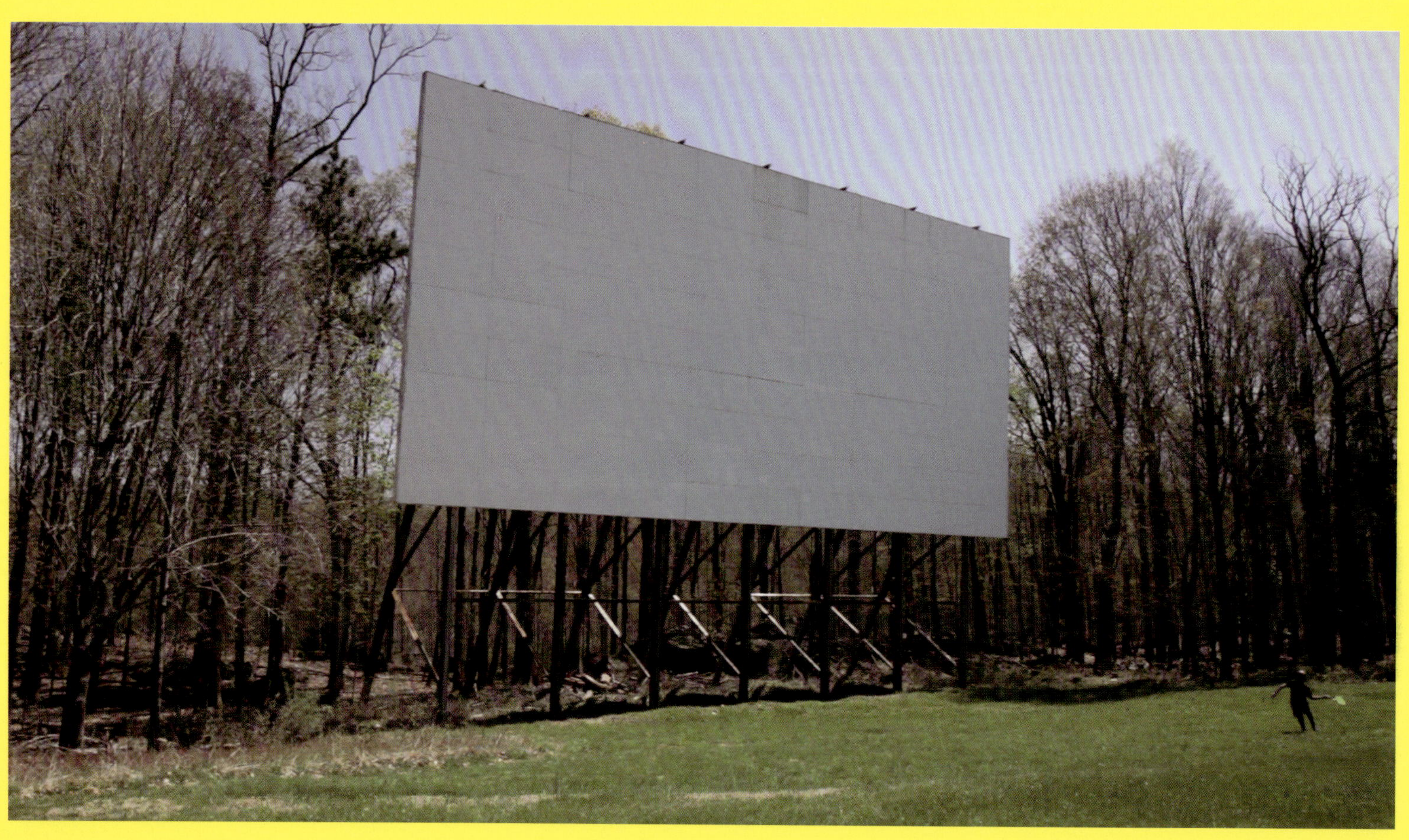

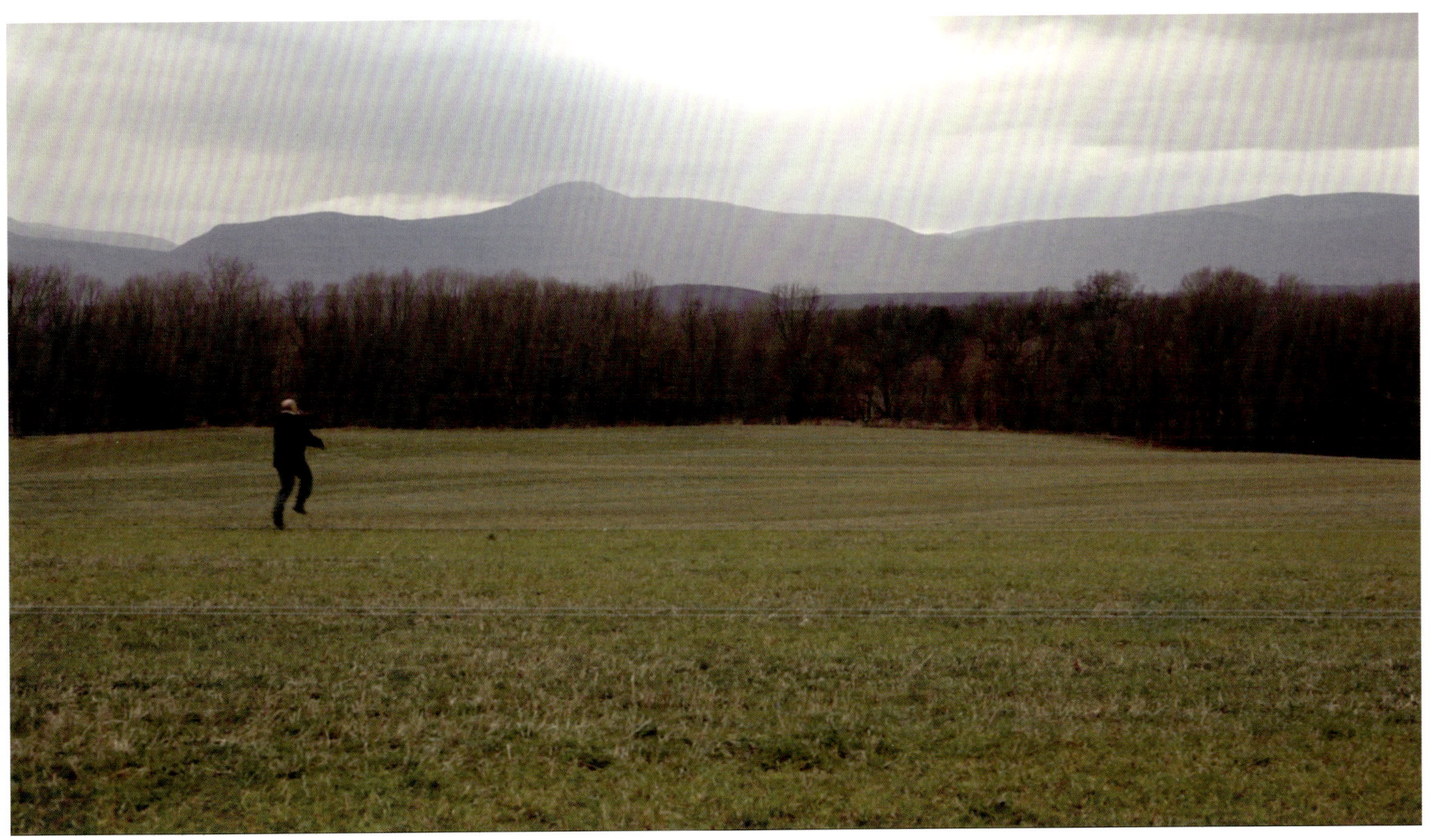

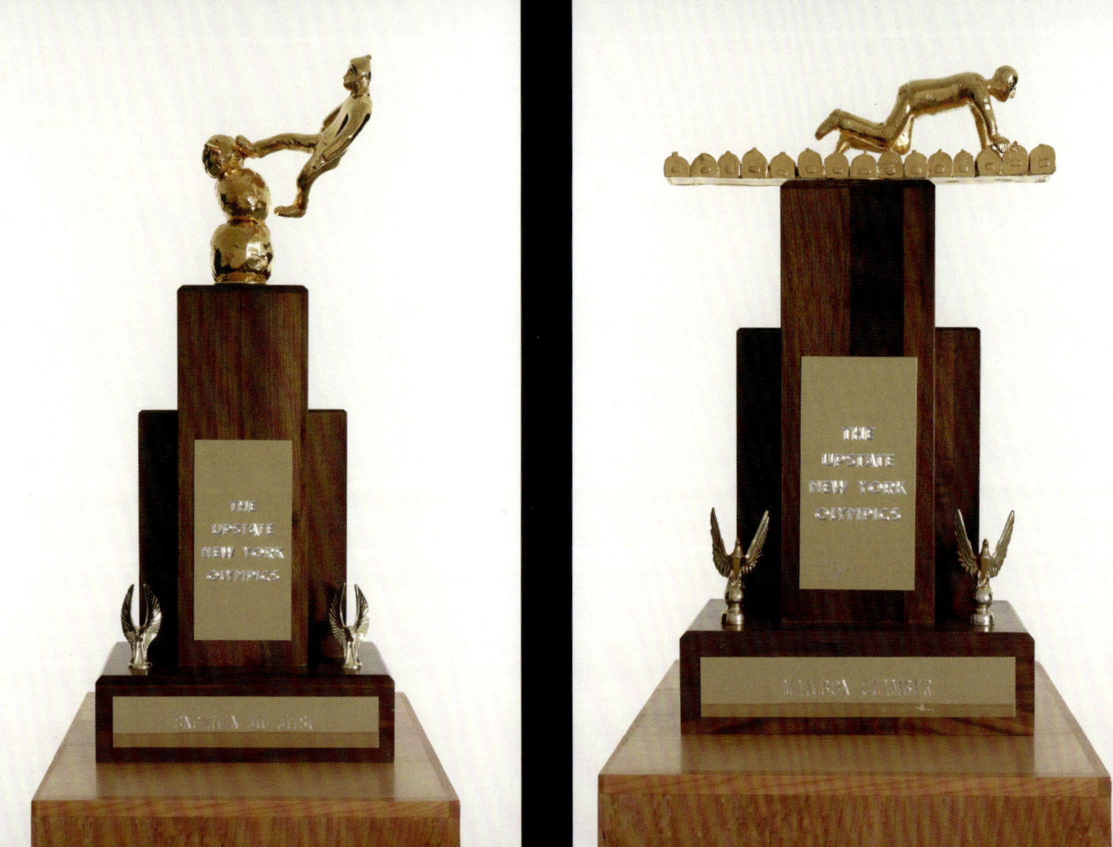
THE
UPSTATE
NEW YORK
OLYMPICS

Foreword

by Sara Pasti

The Hudson Valley is a region that has inspired artists and nourished artistic innovation since the Hudson River School painters traveled upriver in the mid-nineteenth century. The Samuel Dorsky Museum of Art, since its founding in 2001, has celebrated this history of innovation through exhibitions of work by artists who live and create in this region.

The exhibition *The Upstate New York Olympics: Tim Davis* celebrates a contemporary Hudson Valley artist, Tim Davis, who, like his predecessors, draws from the landscape of the region to make his art. The essays contained in this catalogue eloquently and thoughtfully address many aspects of Davis's art making, including his relationship to the landscape—to the "green hills of Upstate New York," as Austin Kelley writes in his essay "Olympic Art." Thomas Bartscherer, in his essay "See the Unseen," writes of Davis that "'Upstate' is what he's interested in. So too were Thomas Cole, Asher Durand and their nineteenth-century cohort. … Davis's New York is by turns more generic and, in its most arresting moments, entirely indigenous, idiosyncratic, hyperlocal." Curator Brian Wallace also addresses the artist's relationship to landscape in his essay by examining the connections that exist between absurdity and profundity in the artist's surroundings and in the actions he performs in them.

Tim Davis is—again like his predecessors—an artist of his time. He uses the contemporary tools of photography, video, and digital imagery to record his vision of the landscape of churches, barns, empty warehouses, and the rural, urban, and suburban neighborhoods of the Hudson Valley. Where the Hudson River School painters saw the region and its pristine beauty through eyes informed by awe and religion, Tim Davis sees the region through a very personal lens. His is a vision shaped by contemporary ideas, artistry, humor, and ingenuity. As with the work of Thomas Cole and Asher Durand, Davis's work changes the way that we see the landscape of the region. Having seen Davis's images, we will never again see a lawn ornament in an Upstate New York yard without imagining Tim jumping over it.

The museum is grateful to the artist for bringing to us this delightful, fun-filled, and—in its own way—awe-inspiring art. We are also grateful to Thomas Bartscherer and Austin Kelley for sharing with us their special understanding of the artist's work. In addition, we thank Jeff Lesperance for his excellent design work, Margaret Vetare for her expert editing, and Dorsey Waxter and Elizabeth Sadeghi from the Greenberg Van Doren Gallery, New York, for their contributions to this catalogue.

Last but not least, we are grateful to the New York State Council for the Humanities for its support of this unique work by a very special Upstate New York artist.

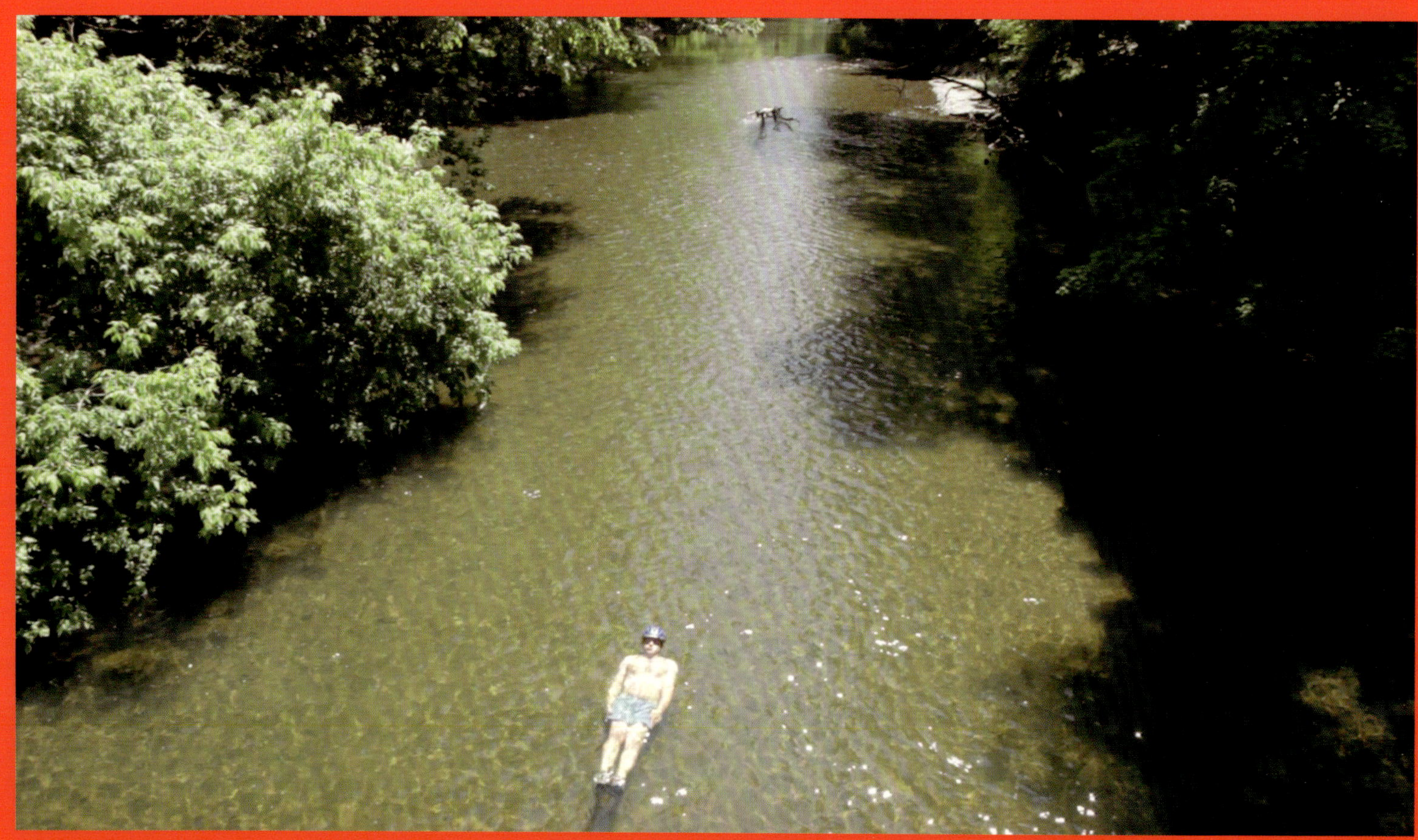

Olympic Art

by Austin Kelley

"I hate the Olympics," Tim Davis told me. "They're embarrassing." Davis is an avid sports fan, but what bothers him about the biennial celebration of curlers and hammer throwers, besides the corporate exploitation, is the gravity bestowed upon minutiae. Irrelevant pursuits are decided by irrelevant details. Judging from the antic, trumped-up sports in Davis's performance collection *The Upstate New York Olympics*—Davis shimmies up public flag poles in *Flag Pole Grapple* and jumps over strangers' ornamental sculptures in *Lawn Jockey Leapfrog*—the artist might prefer some bygone Olympic events from the early twentieth century when the Games were a bit more carnivalesque. There was the rope climb (abandoned after the 1932 Games); the obstacle swim over two boats and then under two boats in the Seine (Paris, 1900); and the plunge for distance (St. Louis, 1904). Like the obstacle swim, the plunge took place only once (1904, St. Louis). American James Dickey won the event when he jumped into a lake and, without moving his arms or legs, hurtled through the water farther than anyone else. If we can tell from old photos, Dickey didn't train very hard. He just let his weight do the work. In Davis's *Upstate* event *Stream Luge* (a reference to the extreme sport of street luge as well as that staple of the winter Olympics), we see the artist, bike-helmeted, floating downstream in the Roeliff Jansen Kill. I can't help but think Davis could have made a great plunger.

Davis would not, however, have medaled in art. Olympic art competitions did take place from 1912 to 1948; gold medals were awarded in categories like architecture and painting, but they were not given to artists who hated the Olympics or thought they were embarrassing, or to artists whose work criticized the culture that supported the Games. Medals were given to works that romanticized sports, like bombastic stadium designs and heroic paintings of wrestlers. Award-winning art had to reflect the ideals of Olympism, the philosophy espoused by Pierre Frédy, Baron de Coubertin, the founder of the modern Olympic Games. Of course, such propagandistic goals—along with the insistence on amateurism—condemned Olympic art to the dustbin of history. Who knew that Stravinsky and Bartók were on the music jury in 1924, or that Olympic medals were awarded for relief sculpture?

Baron de Coubertin, writing under a pseudonym, actually took home the first gold medal in literature (perhaps the fix was in). His triumphant 1912 *Ode to Sport* praised athleticism as the apotheosis of beauty, progress, and justice. Looking back at the gold-medal poem, we can see the contradictions within Olympism. Coubertin wrote, "O Sport, you are Peace! You promote happy relations between peoples." Yet the Olympic project began in part as an embittered reaction to France's defeat in the Franco-Prussian War. Coubertin felt the French had become too effeminate and needed to toughen up physically. He admired battle

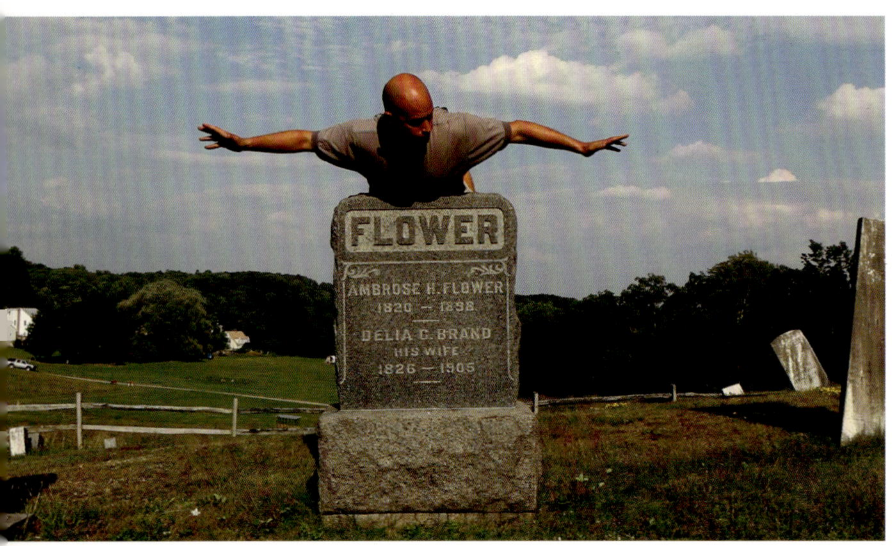

essential purity." As any observer of recent Games knows, we still see the echoes of racial identity or national power, albeit tempered with reverence for training facilities and scientific programs, in Olympic development and preparation programs today. We also still hold up Coubertin's nostalgic ideal of the amateur, even amidst our McDonald's Olympic Happy Meals. The Olympic hero is a good sport who strives for achievement in and of itself. "O Sport," Coubertin wrote, "you appeared suddenly in the midst of the grey clearing which writhes with the drudgery of modern existence, like the radiant messenger of a past age, when mankind still smiled."

Now consider all of this as you watch Tim Davis hang from the roof of a broken-down diner in his *Architectural Ornament Dangle* or balance on the gravestone of a man named Funk in *Headstone Exercises*. Davis is no hero. He evokes Bart Simpson of Springfield, not Homer of Smyrna. He trespasses on others' property. He goofs off. Sometimes his criticism is transparent, as in the first *Upstate New York Olympics* "event," in which the artist looks reverently skyward like a solemn Olympic medalist. Overhead fly the flags of the United States of America, the State of New York, and the McDonald's Corporation. The symbols of nationalism and capitalism, we see right away, will be ridiculed. In *Yard Sign Steam Roller*, Davis literally mows down advertising signs—the papery kind that are stuck in the grass—and in *Church Sign Balance Beam* he attempts to walk on top of biblical exhortations. In each case Davis records sign after unsightly sign, and in the repetition he makes

sports like shooting and fencing, and his Games, as we all know, grew into fiercely nationalistic, politically symbolic contests, not the warm and fuzzy peace summits his poetic rhetoric might lead us to expect. In a similar sense, Coubertin's Olympics were supposedly radically democratic: anyone of any rank could prove biggest, fastest, or strongest. Yet his Olympism was underpinned by a creepy social Darwinism. "Sports strive," Coubertin wrote in the Ode, "towards perfection of the race, destroying unhealthy seed and correcting flaws which threaten its

us see that the landscape is suffused with profoundly flimsy demands on our souls and our wallets.

Another thing which clearly separates Davis's Olympics from Coubertin's is the display of sport itself. Davis isn't a good sport. He isn't really a sport at all. There are no other competitors in *The Upstate New York Olympics*. The rules of the games are not clear; there is no commentary; and there is no real achievement. His events often feature the stripped-down basics of athletic contests. In *Double Barn Ball*, for instance, we immediately understand the challenge: Davis is trying to continually throw two balls on the barn roof without letting either drop to the ground. But they eventually fall, and that's that. Davis deflates all the hoopla that surrounds Olympic toe-pointing and knee-bending and reminds us what we might already know: sports are kind of dumb.

And yet there is something captivating about Davis's performance. It's partly his tongue-in-cheek seriousness and partly the trickster's wink in his eye. He is making it up as he goes, and making a fool of himself, but he's also inventing enticingly purposeless tasks. When we see him play *Drive-in Movie Tennis*, knocking a ball against an enormous white movie screen, the thirteen-year-old inside of us wants to join in. This creative use of space is at the heart of most sports, and is ultimately what makes them compelling.

Then there is the space itself. Tim Davis is above all a pho-

tographer, and he brings his eye for the American landscape to these works. While Davis's subjects are often architectural castoffs like tract housing and dilapidated factories, and we never forget the negative connotations of such spaces, his images are still beautiful. When we watch *Double Barn Ball*, then, we aren't concerned as much with Davis's balls or the problems of the Olympics or the crises of rural life as we are with the striking red barn that looms above. In *Abandoned Building Bowling* Davis rolls a bowling ball inside a rundown factory that glows

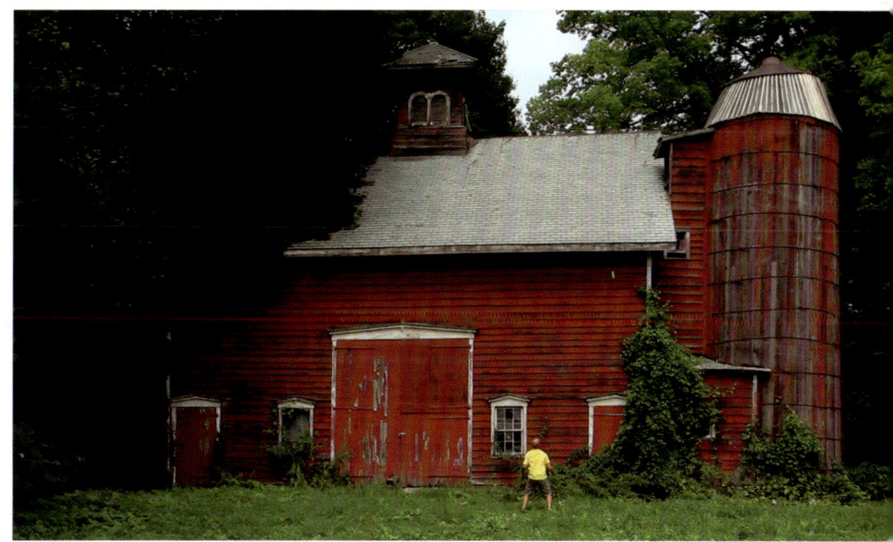

with marvelous blues and shimmering grays. Then he has a go in an empty parking lot beside a giant, lonely industrial plant. The green hills of Upstate New York rise above. There is much referential content here, but there is also pure visual aestheticism coupled with the satisfying sound of bowling balls on tarmac.

The last site in Davis's *Abandoned Building Bowling* is an old, defunct, hoopless basketball gym, a venue that brings us back to athletics and to their architecture. Once in the mid-1990s I watched a sporting event called Rail Jam in New York City's Union Square. It consisted of snowboarders sliding down a railing. Rail Jam derived from skateboarding (which derived from surfing). Skateboarders often make creative and improvisational use of urban or suburban architecture like stairs, railings, or swimming pools. There was nothing creative or improvisational about the official competitive Rail Jam, though, and it hadn't snowed at all. Instead of allowing the event to take place on any real stairs in the cityscape, organizers built a set of moveable metal railings in the urban square and workers sprayed them continually with fake snow. The whole thing was an experiment in simulacra, and I have no doubt that it will become an Olympic sport. Davis's events, by contrast, share the anarchic, outlaw spirit of skateboarding and its authentic interactions with the physical world. Davis plays with the world around him, its rusty pipes and its broken glass, reminding us of the cycle of building and abandoning that is our legacy. The official Olympic Games always take place in spanking new venues, which at each iteration seem to get more audacious and wasteful: giant stadia, glowing water cubes, fake rivers. In the two and a half years since the Games in Beijing, Chinese officials haven't been able to find a good use for their show-stopping Bird's Nest Stadium. Now they're considering turning it into a shopping mall. Perhaps it won't be long before Davis will break in, bowling ball in hand.

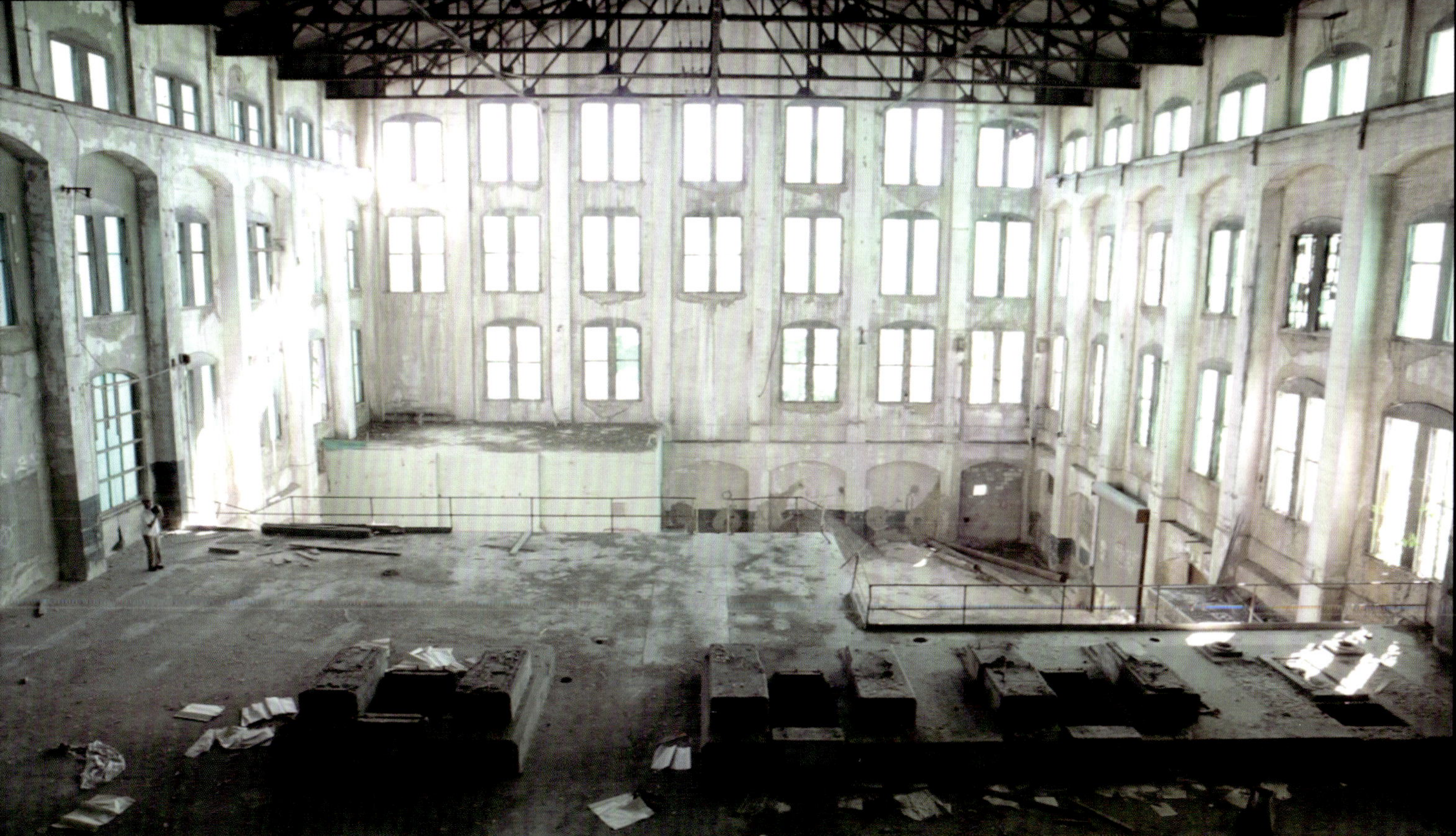

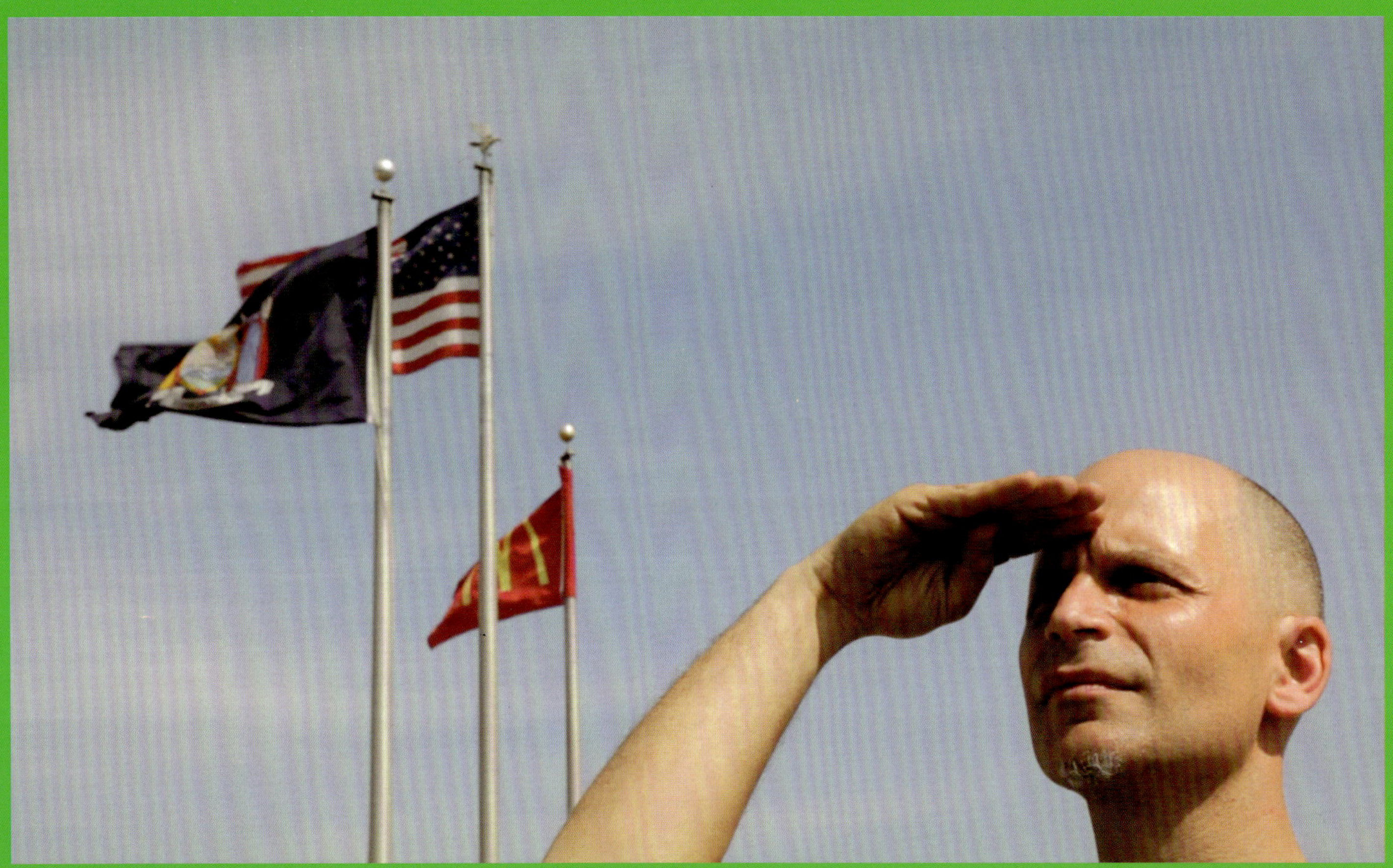

See the Unseen

by Thomas Bartscherer

The Olympics are for Tim Davis what Homer's *Odyssey* was for James Joyce: a conceit, a loose set of rules that structure serious play. Davis has a dual role in *The Upstate New York Olympics*. As hero of the film, he's a cross between Quixote and Buster Keaton, journeying through suburbs and semirural regions, competing solo in events with names like *Long Distance Skip*, *Cross Country Basketball,* and *Gravestone Hurdle*. Davis the cameraman, meanwhile, has neoclassical sensibilities: balance, clarity, restraint, simplicity. The pictures are poised, the color bright, his eye for detail unerring. Taken as a whole, the work is about the place named in its title, the time of its making, and the adventure still possible—even now, even here—for a good sport with good eyes. Like Joyce's *Ulysses*, *The Upstate New York Olympics* portrays a fallen world but rallies comedy against nostalgia and defeats cynicism with fleeting revelations of a beauty as unexpected as it is inexplicable.

In the title sequence, the background is clear blue sky. The artist—call him the Athlete—stands in the foreground. Three flags, behind him to the left, flap in the wind; music plays; it is the Olympic medal ceremony. But in this version, the American flag is flanked on one side by the flag of the State of New York and on the other by the Golden Arches of the McDonald's Corporation. The athlete is alone and his raised hand neither covers his heart nor extends overhead in triumph. It is instead brought to his brow, shading his eyes as if in salute, or rather, as if he were looking for something.

The flags give a hint. That an American artist would look to, or for, New York is commonplace. But Davis's New York is not the big metropolis. "Upstate" is what he's interested in. So too were Thomas Cole, Asher Durand, and their nineteenth-century cohort. But Davis isn't after sweeping vistas of pristine nature. Nor is he, like a more recent generation, documenting the points of contact and commerce between upstate and the city: the Hudson River, the railroad, the heirloom tomatoes and heritage pigs that supply Manhattan's markets. Davis's New York is by turns more generic and, in its most arresting moments, entirely indigenous, idiosyncratic, hyperlocal.

The McDonald's flag signals the generic theme. On one level, this work calls attention to the demise of local specificity as American architecture and culture become increasingly standardized in the postwar decades. Consider, for example, the first event after the title sequence. Even before the name of the event appears on the screen, we know—but how?—that the structure we're looking at is, or rather was, a bowling alley. No sign identifies it, nor is there a synecdochic ball or pin to tip us off. But when the title of the event does appear—*Abandoned Building Bowling*—and then the Athlete enters at the far left of the screen and rolls a bowling ball as if down a lane that runs the length of the building, clear across the horizontal plane of the still frame, the joke works in part because we have already recognized this as a bowling alley. Like the diner or the drive-in cinema or the motel that appear in other sequences, this is the architectural vernacular of suburban and subrural America in the second half of the twentieth century, which, taken to the extreme, is manifested in the generic franchise design of nationwide chains like McDonald's.

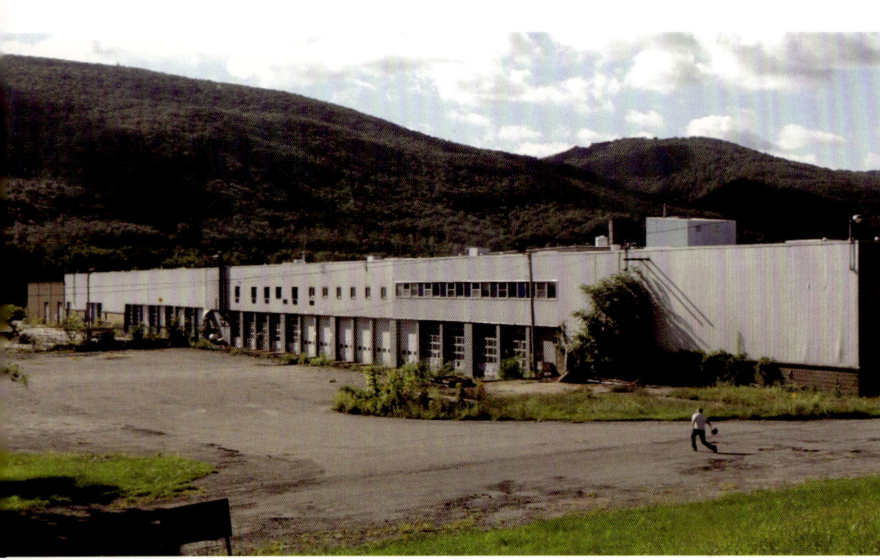

The Upstate New York Olympics has a critical strain, somewhat in the spirit of Marx (Groucho, if not Karl). It's slapstick satire. One target is the modern Olympic movement, which in the name of internationalism often ignores, distorts, even destroys indigenous natural and cultural landscapes. Davis's games, by contrast, are proudly parochial, disclosing and celebrating local color. Yet the small world he depicts with such sensitivity to detail is not spared the satirist's barbs. One of the funniest sequences begins with the Athlete bounding out from behind a bush to leapfrog a lawn jockey statuette adorning the front yard of a nondescript suburban home. There is a quick cut to another yard with another lawn jockey, which the Athlete also leaps. And then another and another and another. This is the stuff of screwball comedy, but there's also a critical edge. Dark skinned lawn jockeys, often bearing the exaggerated features of racial caricature, were once commonplace, and although they are rare these days, a couple of black-faced jockeys do show up, like the return of the repressed, in *Lawn Jockey Leapfrog*. Class is also at play here, the jockey being emblematic of a kind of luxury unavailable to many who display the emblem in front of their modest homes. And then of course there is the undertone of nostalgia for an idealized past, some lost age of gentility. As the segment continues and the number of jumped jockeys nears two score, this peculiar icon begins to look increasingly like the symptom of cultural pathology. In another direction altogether, the work is a satirical play on the image of the American artist as a kind of action hero: think Jackson Pollock, Richard Serra, Matthew Barney. Taking this mythology to the absurd, here

comes Davis cast as an Olympian grappling with industrial
material in *Rusty Pipe Drag* or clawing his way through a pile
of rotting vegetables in *Compost Freestyle*.

But critique is at most a subtext in this work. Davis is too curious, too exuberant, too enamored. And his game is not fixed.
It matters that actual skill, albeit modest, is required for some
events, and that there is the occasional risk of bodily harm,
which, if not serious, is nonetheless real. The Athlete is putting
something of himself on the line, not merely pretending to do
so. Likewise, the transgressive element of these exploits is
crucial. One ought not to climb the village flag pole or hurdle
over gravestones or trespass on private property. But such is
the way of comedy. The infractions are minor, meant not to
shatter, but rather to open a crack through which something
can be shown and seen.

Take the event called *Church Sign Balance Beam*. Like *Lawn
Jockey Leapfrog*, it's based on serial observation reminiscent of
the work of Bernd and Hilla Becher. It comprises, in effect, an incipient
typology of church signs, from the cheap, portable metal kind to the
rustic wood-framed version to imposing structures of brick or stone.
Some make requests, others make announcements, many quote the
Bible. Walking across the thin tops of these signs—the balancing act—
demands agility, and the feat courts danger of minor injury. The irreverence of the trespass also has a hint of risk—one imagines parishioners
emerging with pitchforks—but it might just as well occasion reflection. Is

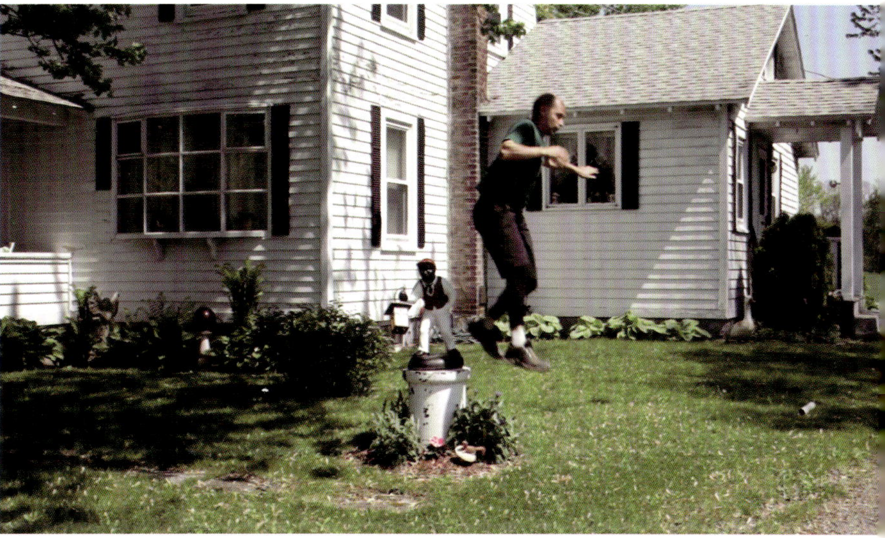

scripture as marketing slogan not itself a kind of irreverence?

Quite apart from all that is the strange poetics of found language in
this sequence, which resonates with the spirit of perpetual discovery
that animates the work as a whole. "A mother understands what a child
does not say," reads the sign in front of the First Reformed Church
of Bethlehem, founded in 1763. Another quotes the prophet Isaiah,
promising renewed strength for "those who wait on the Lord." And St.

Mark's Lutheran Church invites, indeed, exhorts us to "see the unseen."

At one point during another Upstate New York Olympics event, a passer-by calls out from off-screen, "Why photograph the ugly when you can photograph the beautiful?" It's a chance encounter, but the man's question goes to the heart of this whole project. The answer is right on the surface. Why does Tim Davis photograph a roadside pond covered in scum? Because somewhere on his journey unexpectedly he came upon this broad expanse of voluptuous green, like a color field canvas painted by the hand of nature. Because he noticed that when he skips a stone across it, the repeated impacts describe a receding series of black marks on the surface, like cuts in the canvas, revealing the water below just for an instant before the thick green flora oozes back and his mark disappears. Because, like much in this work, it is beautiful.

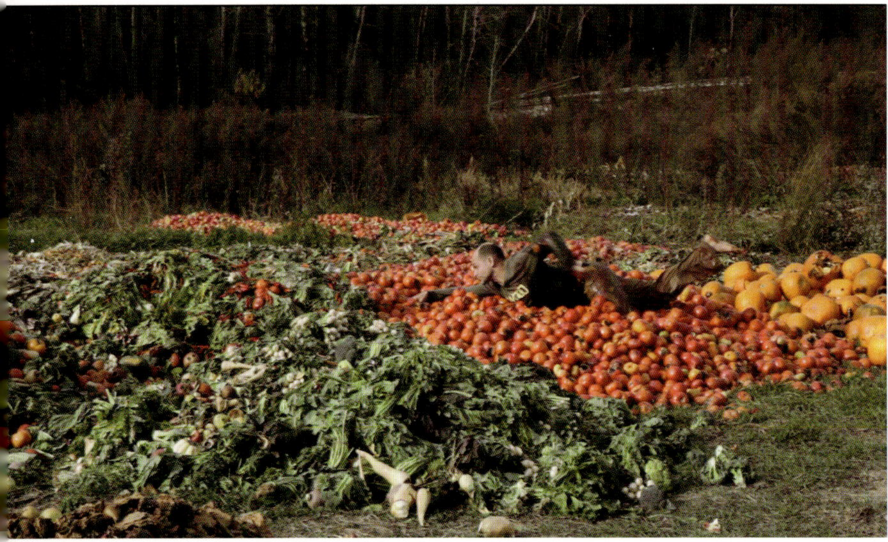

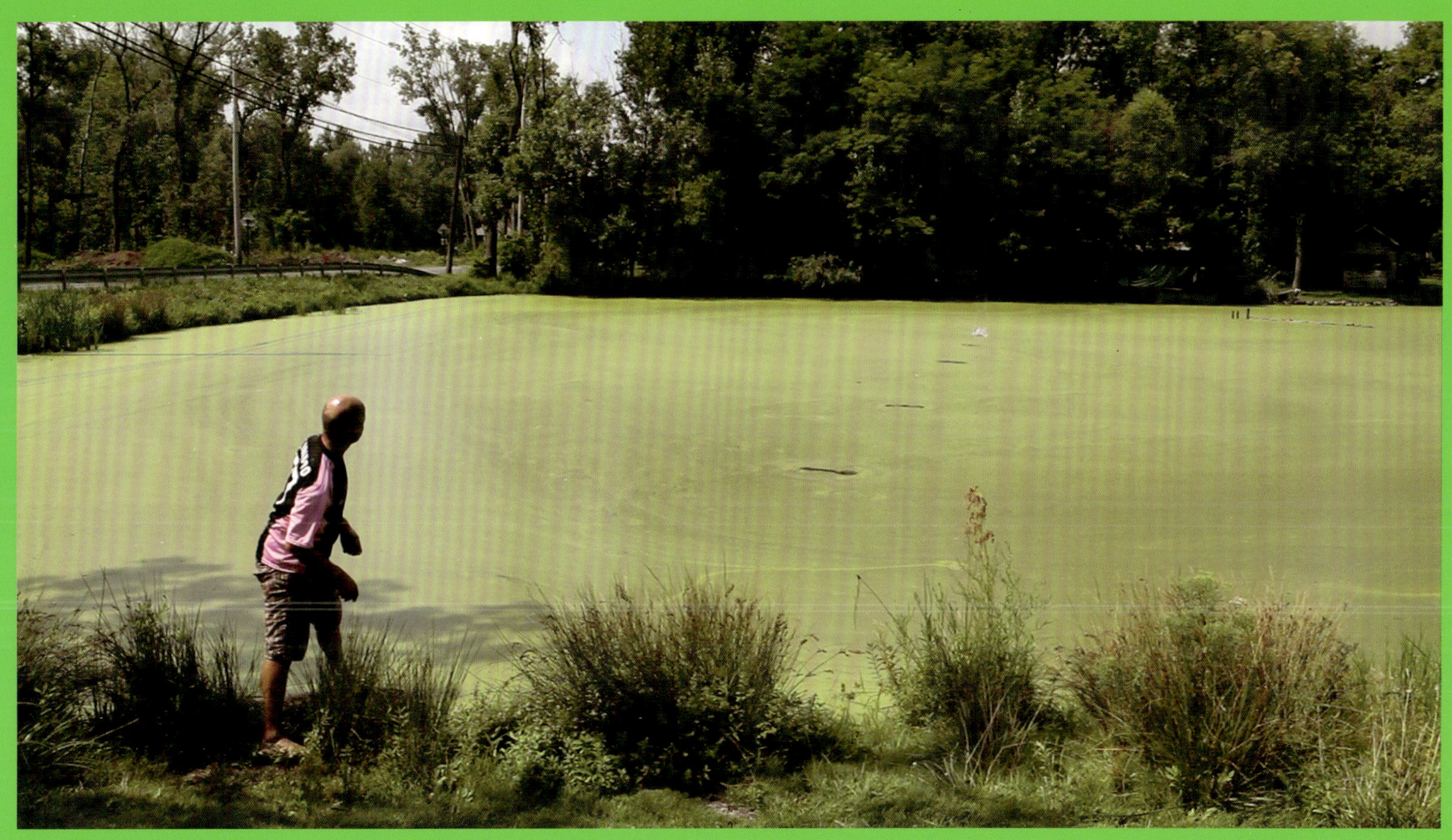

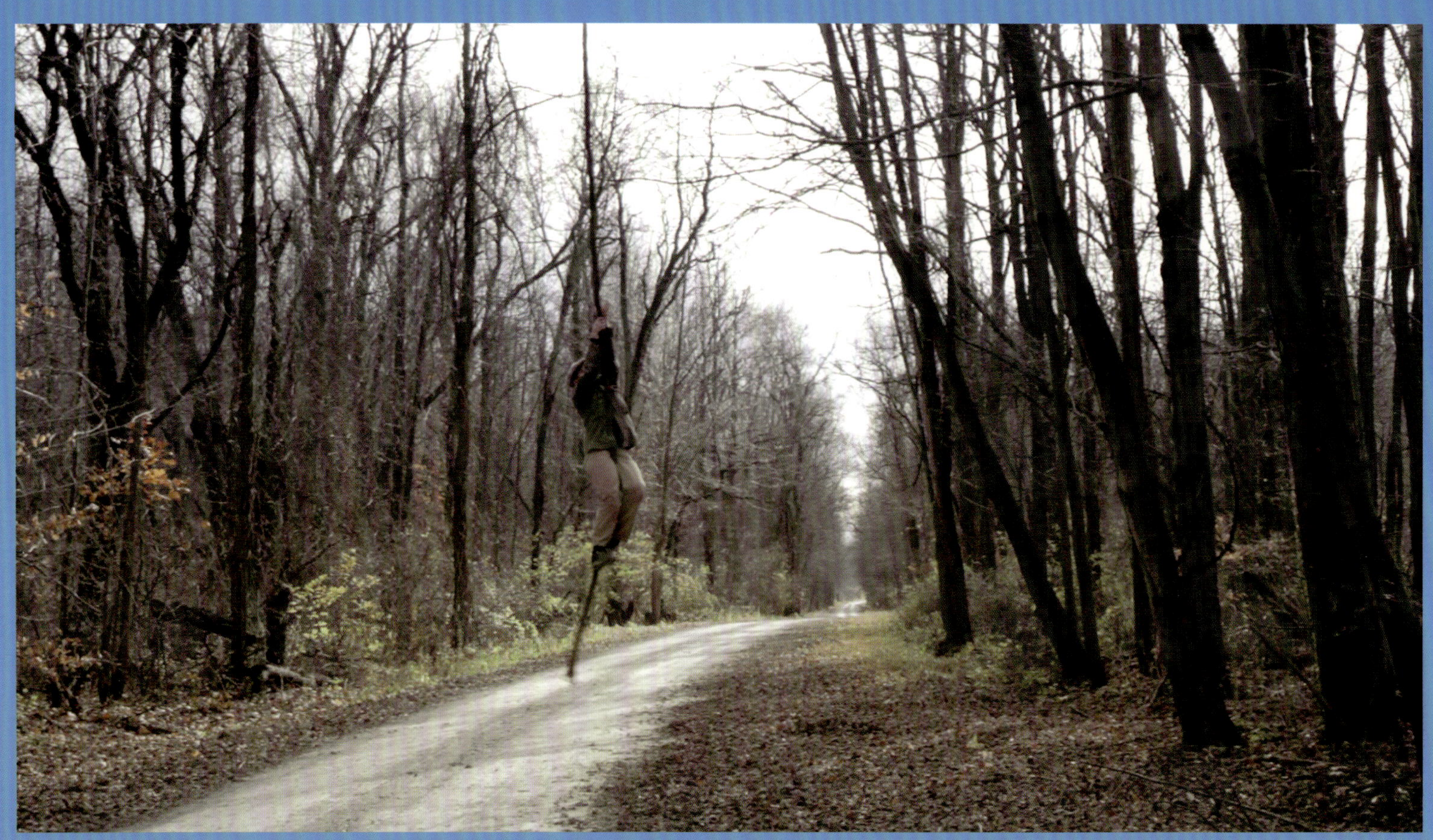

"From the Sublime to the Ridiculous"

by Brian Wallace

"From the sublime to the ridiculous." The phrase comes into my head as I'm looking at a work-in-progress sampling of Tim Davis's *Upstate New York Olympics* videos in the middle of a loud open studio/party given back in October by Tim and his wife, the painter Lisa Sanditz. I sit on a hard chair with my partner and watch nearly an hour of rough-cut edited footage. People come and go or stay and sit, watching two or four or seven or eight events, laughingly noting the controlled energy of Tim's antic actions and the attention-grabbing but commonplace scenarios into which they are set.

I know Davis's photographic work well, and I thought I had become accustomed to the slyly provocative and beauty-riddled way he combines form and subject matter to undermine the trustworthiness of these key components of visual expression. In *Permanent Collection*, the first body of his work that I saw, light obscures the subject by becoming the subject, occluding topical content while revealing—by reveling in—the perceptual aspects of looking. In the more recent *My Life in Politics* and the earlier *Retail*, subject matter conditionally pins together about-to-fall-apart compositions; at the same time, the anxiety brought on by images shot at not quite the decisive moment heightens the urgent banality of the subjects. Even the lyrical works Davis made during a collaborative project involving the Dorsky and Historic Huguenot Street can be understood, ultimately, in terms of complementary form and narrative. These site-specific photographs record objects and spaces and the tension between them by refusing to prioritize subject over background and refusing to emphasize center over periphery. While the photographs enunciate the terms of, rather than simply record, encounters between a fundamentally curious photographer and a deeply resistant site—they don't let themselves be read very easily—in the end, they do allow for the possibility that the contradictions they set out can be resolved.

As I view the *Upstate New York Olympics* pieces, though, I find myself surprised by the vast distance between the weirdly elegant timbre and the wiseacre affect of both the compositions I'm seeing and the subject matter I'm watching. "From the sublime to the ridiculous." A slight man—the artist—vaults, somewhat awkwardly, onto the narrow top of a disturbingly flimsy sign advertising a church; sign and artist tremble as an equilibrium is

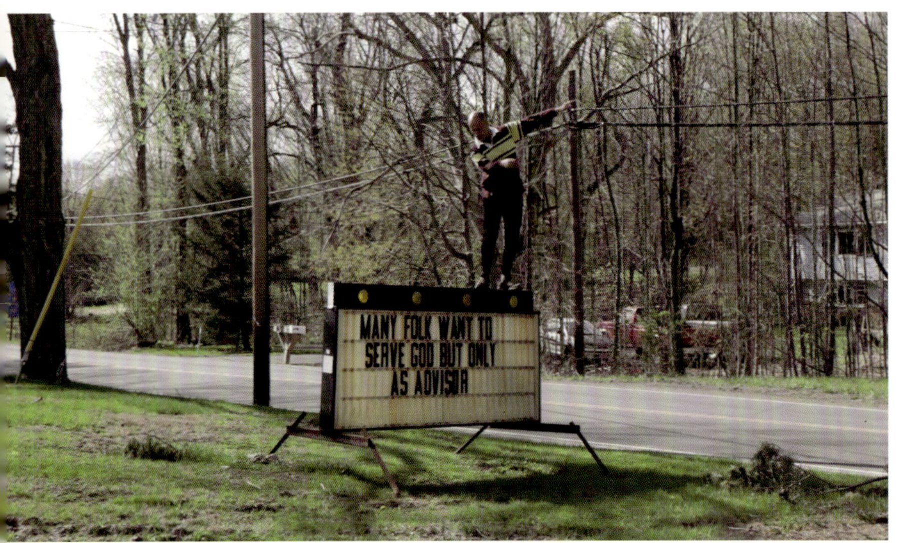

neighbor or the minister. Next I see, not another competitor's attempt at perfection—as I would in the televised and proper Olympics—but this casually attired quasi-athlete's stab at traversing another, not-quite-different-enough-to-be-interesting church sign. This happens again, and then again. All the while, around this action, picture-postcard villages arrange themselves into perfect compositions, and shiny cars pass by occasionally on meticulously striped roads.

"The sublime" and "the ridiculous." Tom Paine and Napoleon Bonaparte are each credited with founding variations on the familiar expression. Paine, in "The Age of Reason" (1795), notes that "One step above the sublime, makes the ridiculous; and one step above the ridiculous, makes the sublime again." Napoleon, by contrast, returning to Paris from Russia on a sledge, dryly characterized (in a letter to Polish Ambassador Abbé De Pradt) his mammoth 1812 loss of army and empire as having gone but one step "from the sublime to the ridiculous." Paine, the definitive democrat, levels the two terms with

sought, found, lost, and found again. The artist—he's healthy, but hardly Olympian in stature—traverses the sign hesitantly, evincing the intense focus of the high-level gymnast but none of the discipline (or sequins) needed to compete at that level. The dismount is accomplished, shakily, with apologetic self-deprecation, not the perky exuberance of victory or the grim smile of defeat. When he finishes, I feel a sense of relief: not the expansive relief at the conclusion of a great performance, but relief that he didn't break the church sign or hurt himself or get yelled at by a a deliberately pedestrian, procedural formulation, while Bonaparte, the despot's despot, heightens the difference between the two words in order to dramatize his own rise and fall. Davis (I begin to see that this work *is* connected to his own past projects) is in Paine's camp. While his works do encompass an extremely disparate set of strategies and subjects, the span in them between aspiration and reality brings the sublime and the ridiculous into a meaningful relationship.

Davis began this body of work—a series of videos documenting the artist performing variations on traditional sporting activities—the day after his 40th birthday as a response to his sense of his changing relationships, as a man and as an artist, to key aspects of the culture in which he operates.

When I recently asked Davis directly about the impetus behind this project, he said to me that he was struck by a combined admiration for and loathing of what his age forces him to see as the next generation's sense of place in the world. He cautiously broached the example of the "Jackass" series of videos and movies as an admirably direct—albeit deliberately non-contemplative—expression of profoundly fraught relationships with the physical world. He also referred to his ongoing interest in the self-effacing—but deeply confident—humor of early West Coast video art by practitioners such as William Wegman and Bruce Naumann, both of whom address mortality, endurance, power, and responsibility with an absurd literalness of narrative and a perverse economy of technical/formal means.

The actions Davis has chosen to perform—homemade, humorous, yet humdrum riffs on ur-sport events—and the deadpan manner in which he completes (as distinct from "competes in") them also convey an exhaustion with the corporate, uniformed, rule-bound, success-oriented spectacles of international sport. Davis challenges the soft drink-sponsored platitudes and credit card-and-airline-funded verities of the so-called Olympic move-ment with direct actions in familiar settings yielding humble outcomes.

Along with these notions of gender, physicality, and ethics, the artist is also acutely aware of the ways in which the landscape—and artists' and viewers' ways of looking at and occupying the landscape—features prominently in this body of work. The initial compositions in each of the videos in Davis's project—the view, without artist/performer—refer to particular schools of art. Each school is made up of an agreed-upon

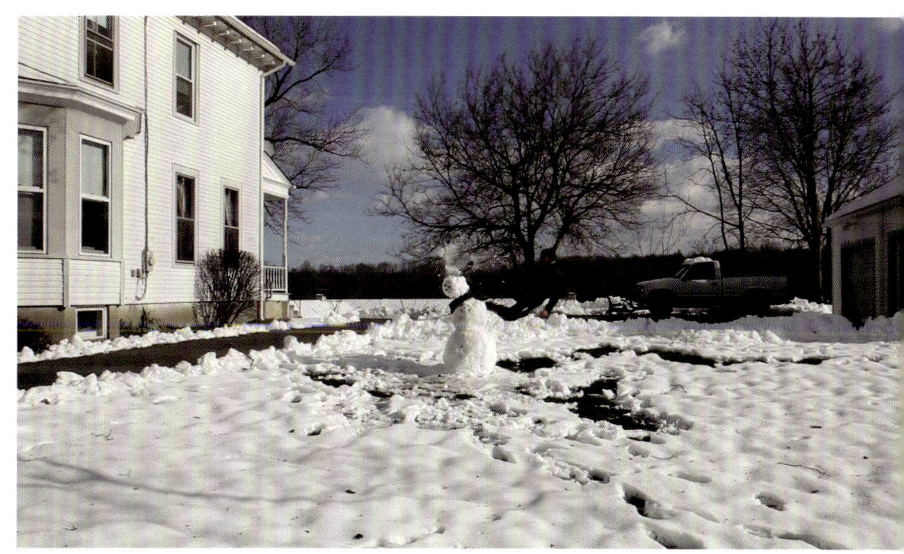

set of visual conventions, ranging from the products of the self-styled Hudson River School to the aestheticized typologies of Stephen Shore. Sublime? Yes: natural vistas, physical challenges, imminent dangers, references to the infinite, Ridiculous? Yes: silly, amusing, not at all sensible, unreasonable. Inspiring scornful pity.

The earnestness of Davis's own sport-like actions mirrors, and also slyly undercuts, the seriousness of these endeavors. This earnestness, on the other hand, also draws the viewer's attention to the economy—in two senses of the word—of the scenes depicted in Davis's videos. We see fading towns, closed factories, downsized homes, and abandoned items and in-transition properties of all kinds. But we also see a scene that is, in the artist's words, "under-seen"—that is, viewscapes full of content for new viewers to use as fodder for fresh thinking and fresh action. There is an optimism to the empty frames of Davis's compositions that both invites and undercuts what has come to be seen as the typically American response to (seemingly) empty space: it'd be wrong not to fill this with something. "One step above the sublime, makes the ridiculous; and one step above the ridiculous, makes the sublime again."

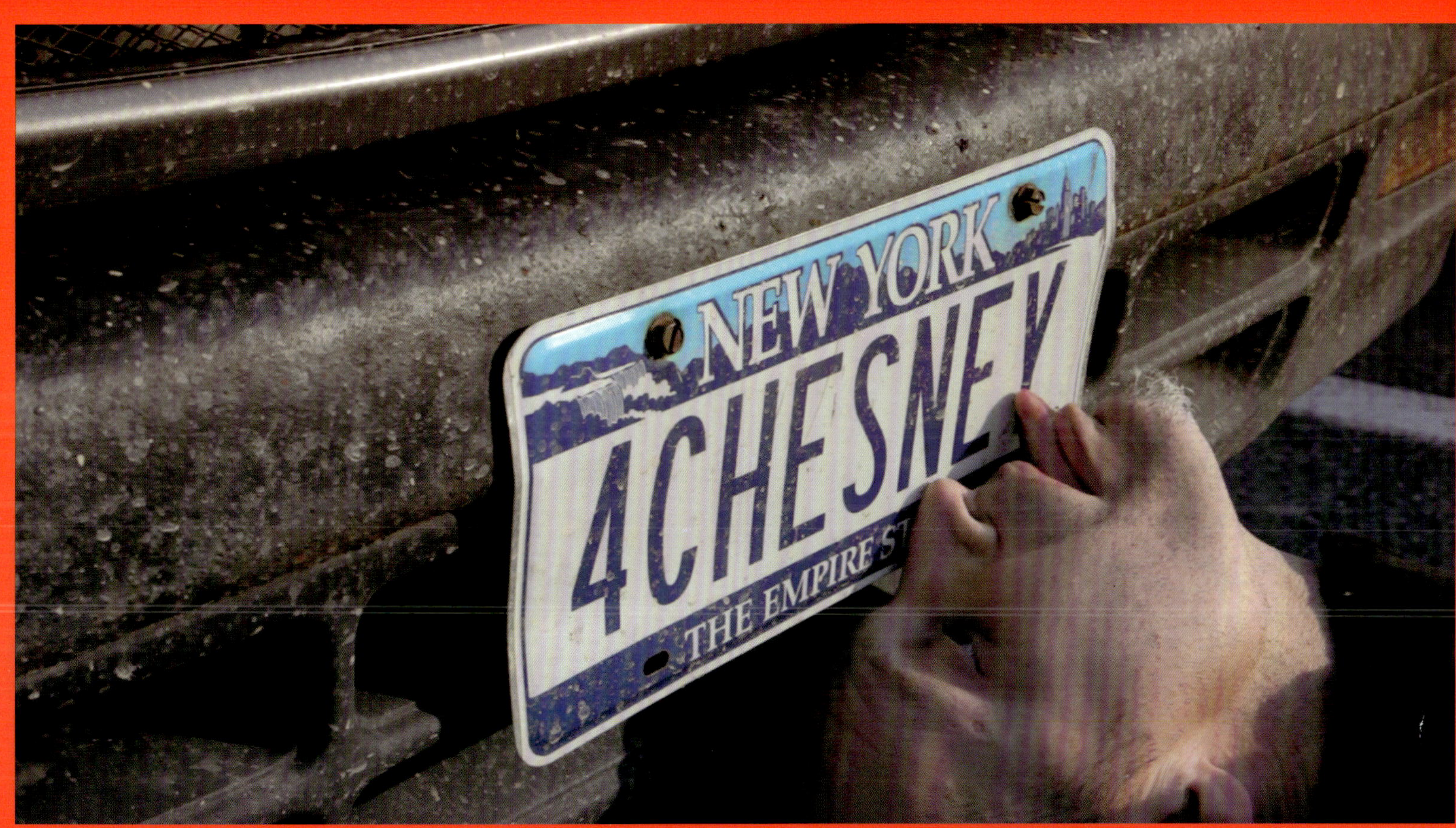

NEW YORK
4CHESNEY
THE EMPIRE ST

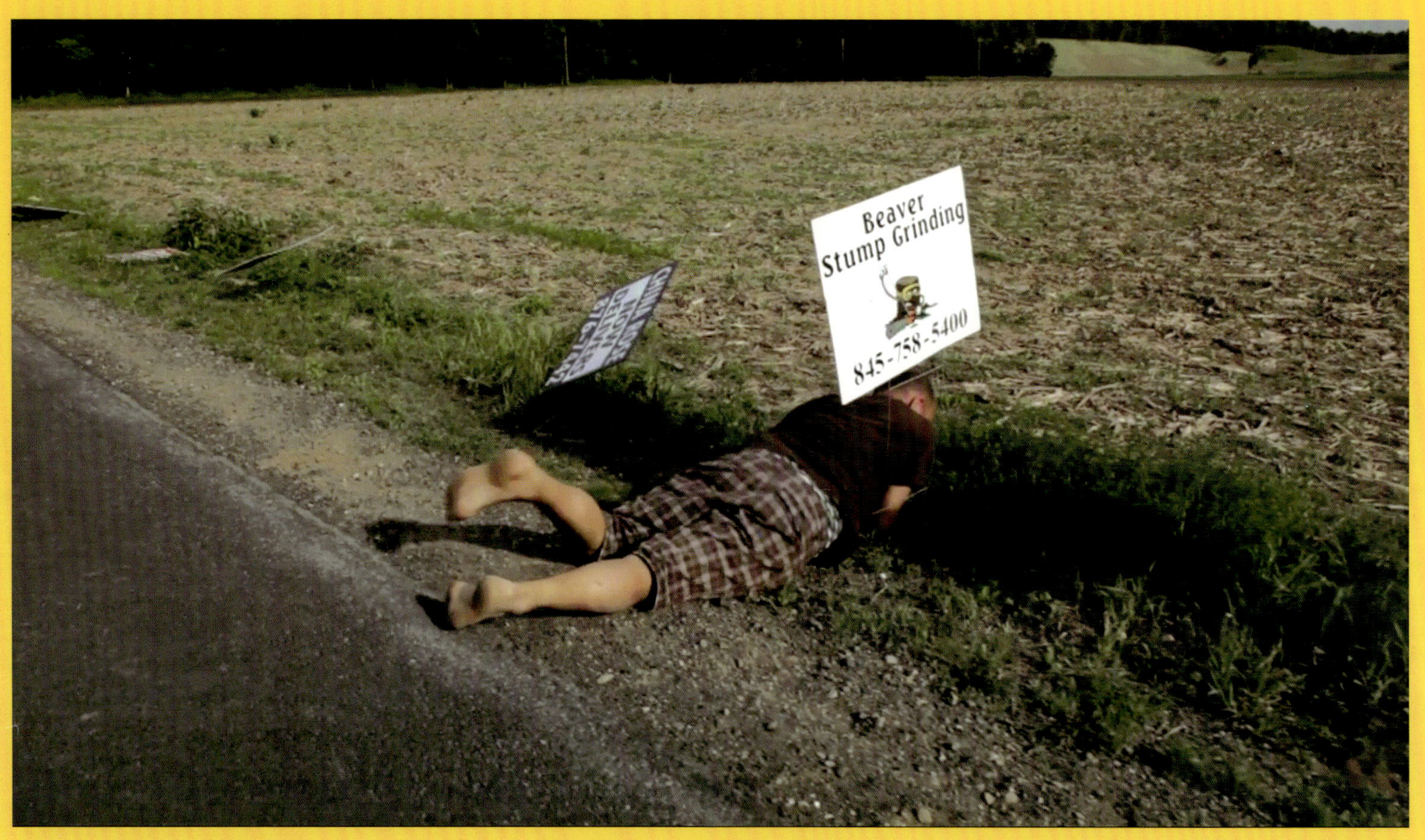

Beaver
Stump Grinding
845-758-5400

PORTFOLIO

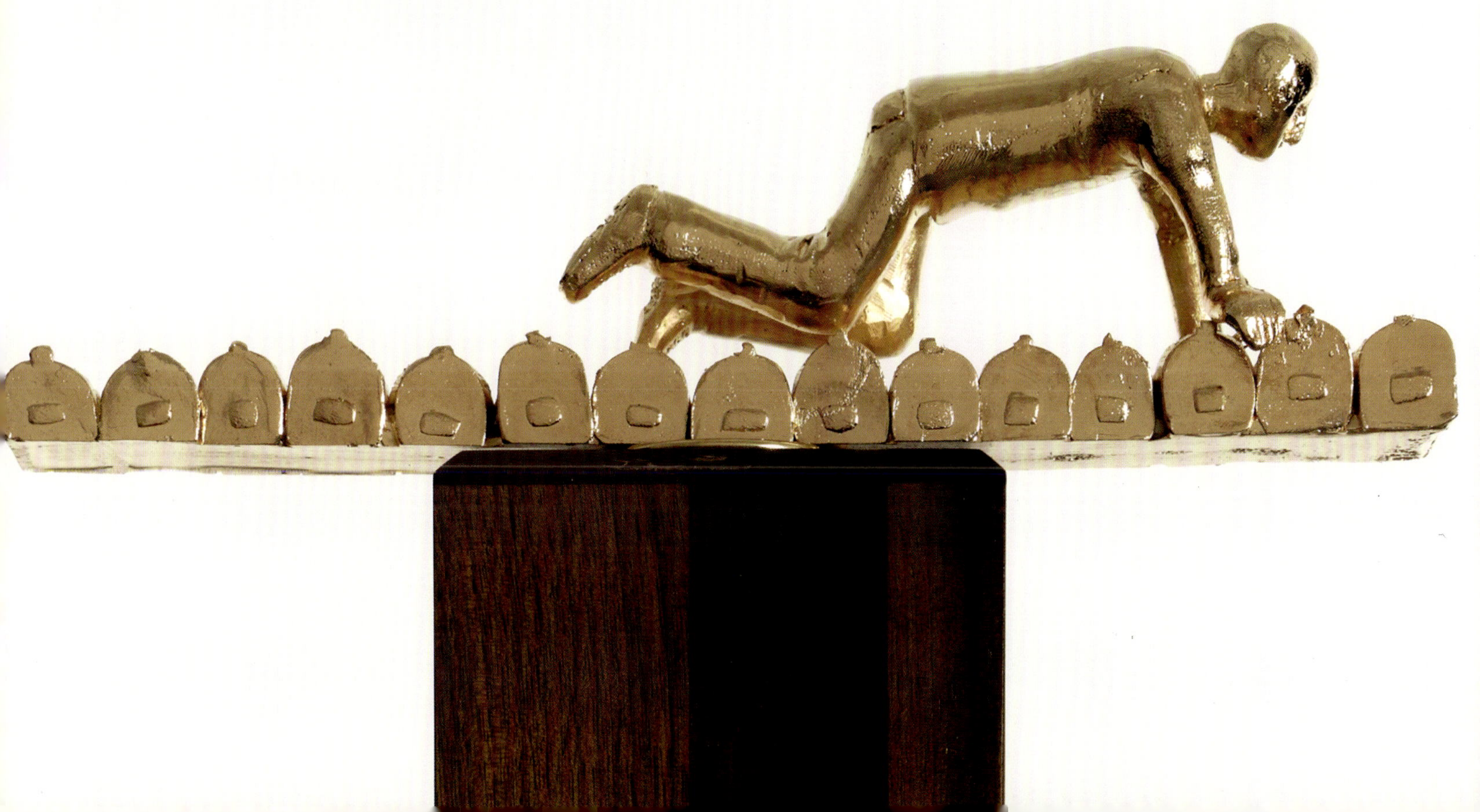

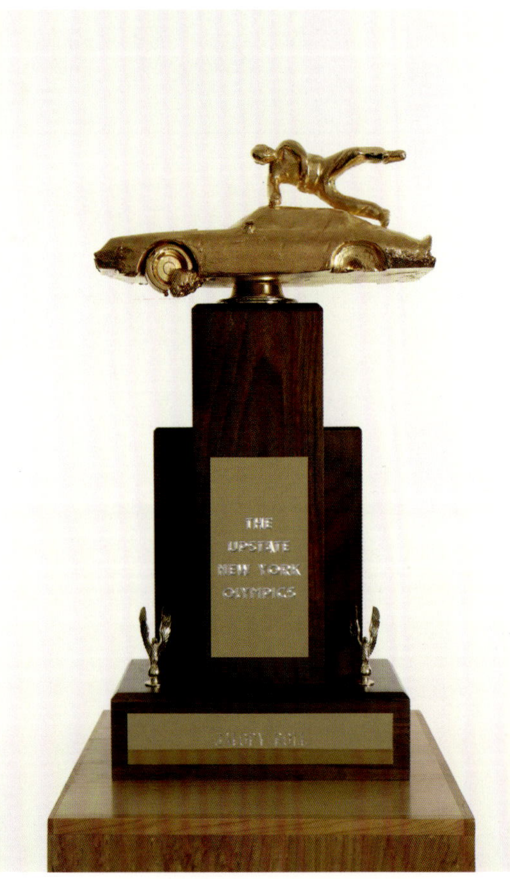

THE
UPSTATE
NEW YORK
OLYMPICS

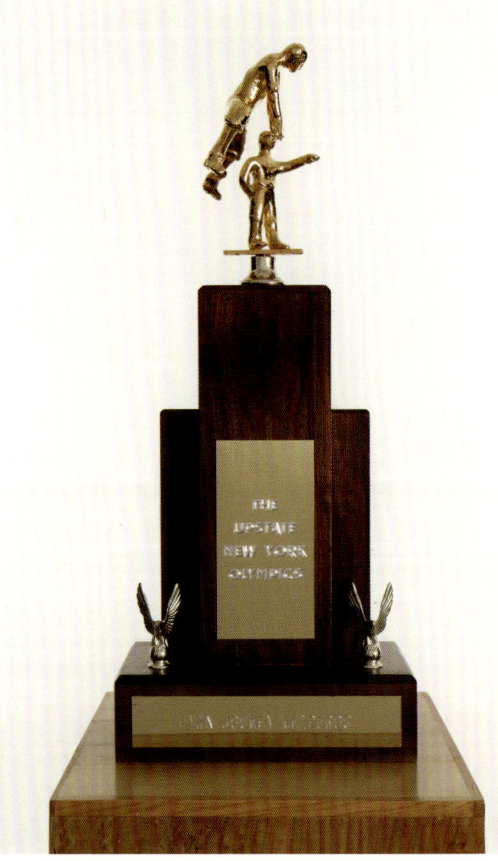

THE
UPSTATE
NEW YORK
OLYMPICS

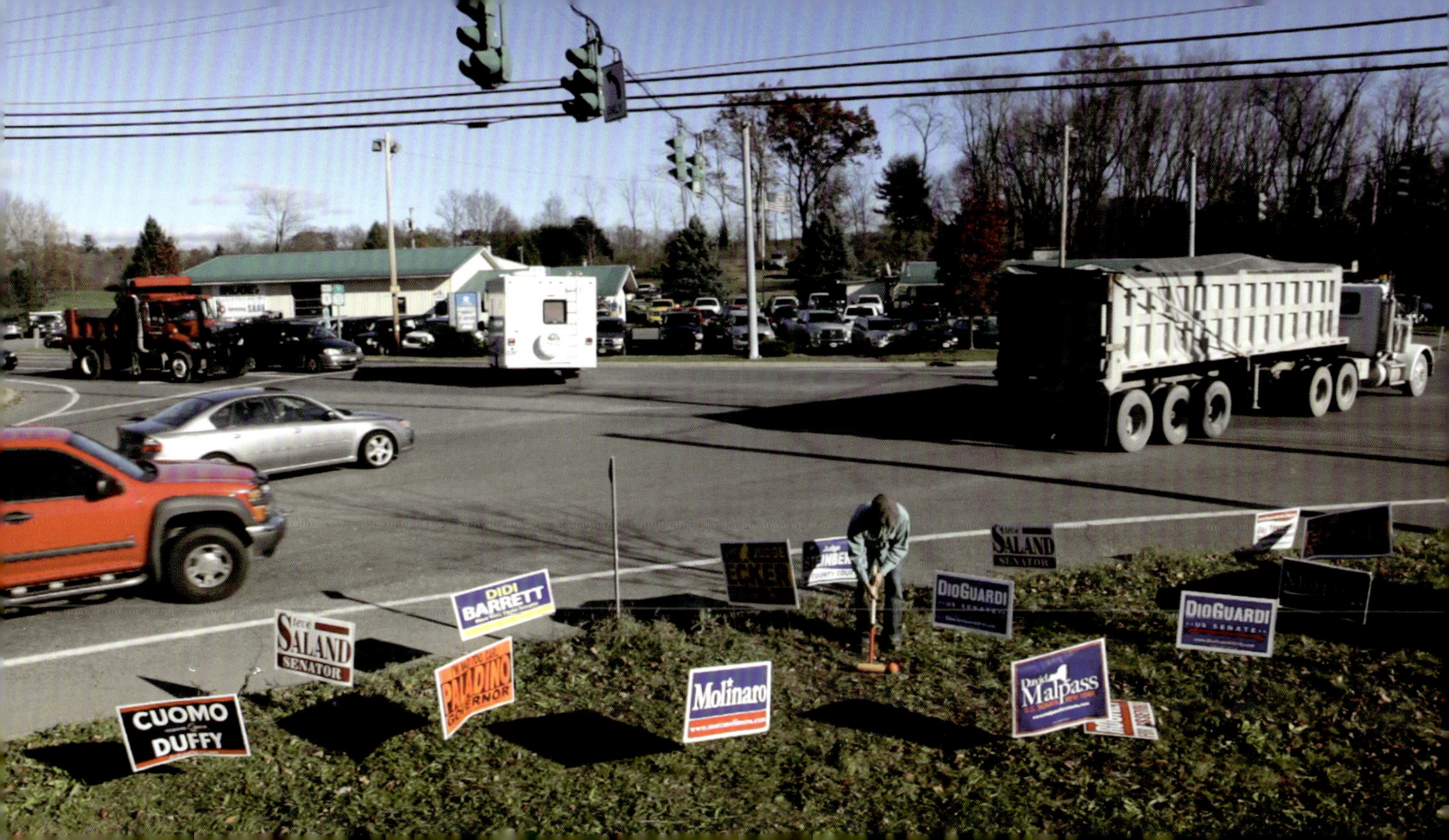
Steve SALAND SENATOR
DIDI BARRETT
CUOMO DUFFY
PALADINO GOVERNOR
Molinaro
Judge ECKER
Judge STEINBERG COUNTY COURT
SALAND SENATOR
DioGuardi US SENATE
DioGuardi US SENATE
David Malpass

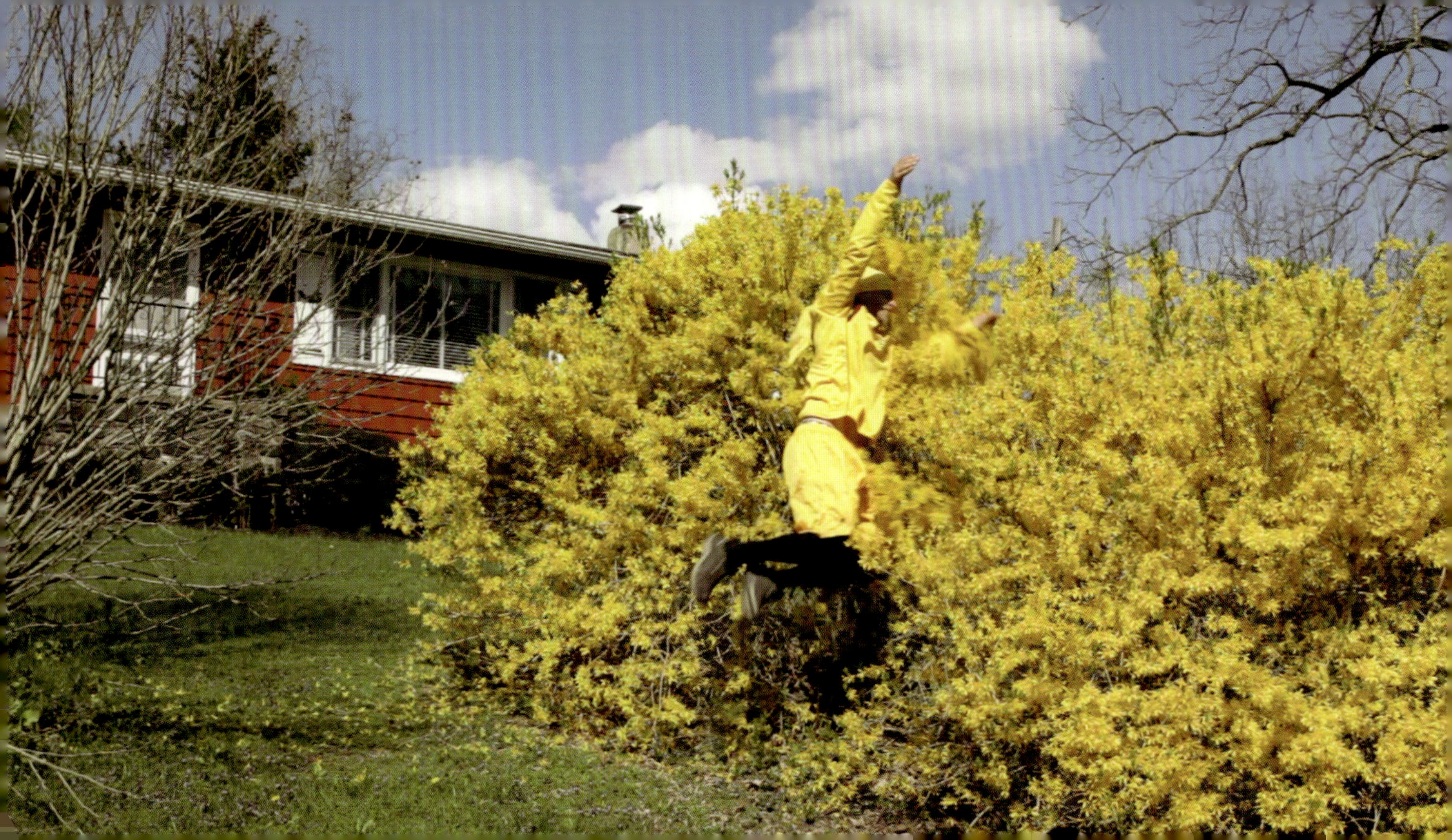

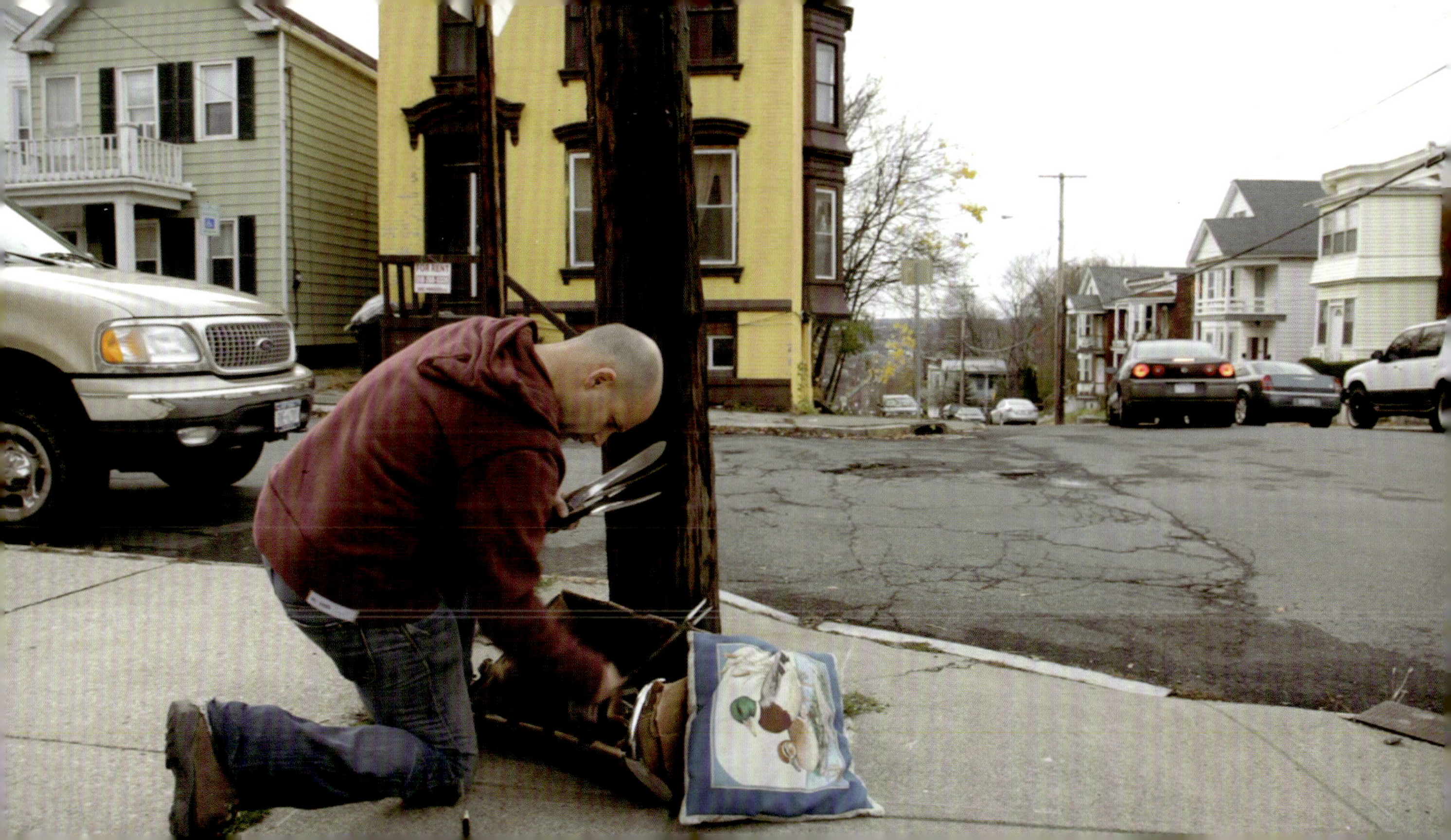

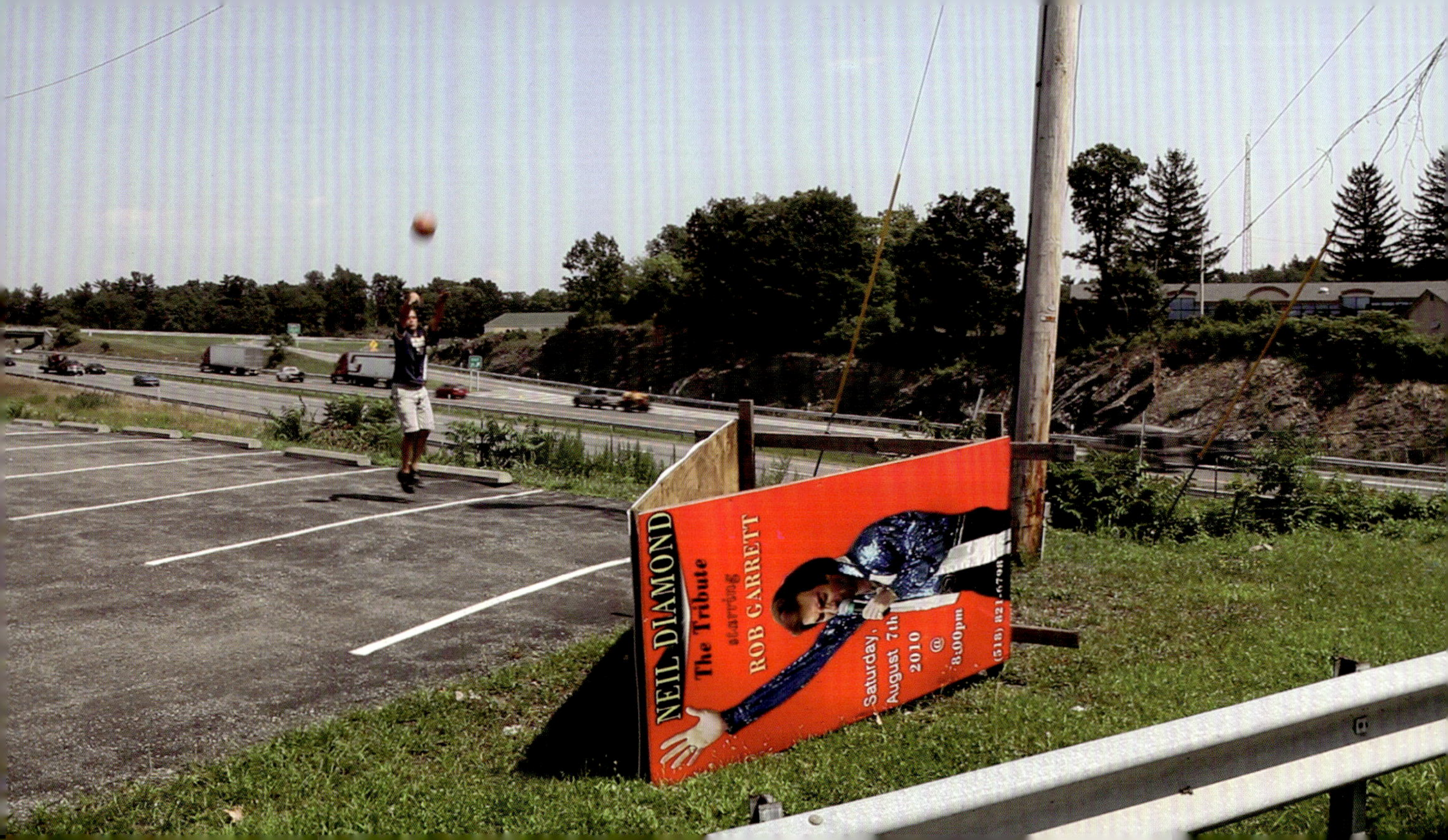

NEIL DIAMOND
The Tribute
starring
ROB GARRETT
Saturday,
August 7th
2010
@
8:00pm
(518) 821-6798

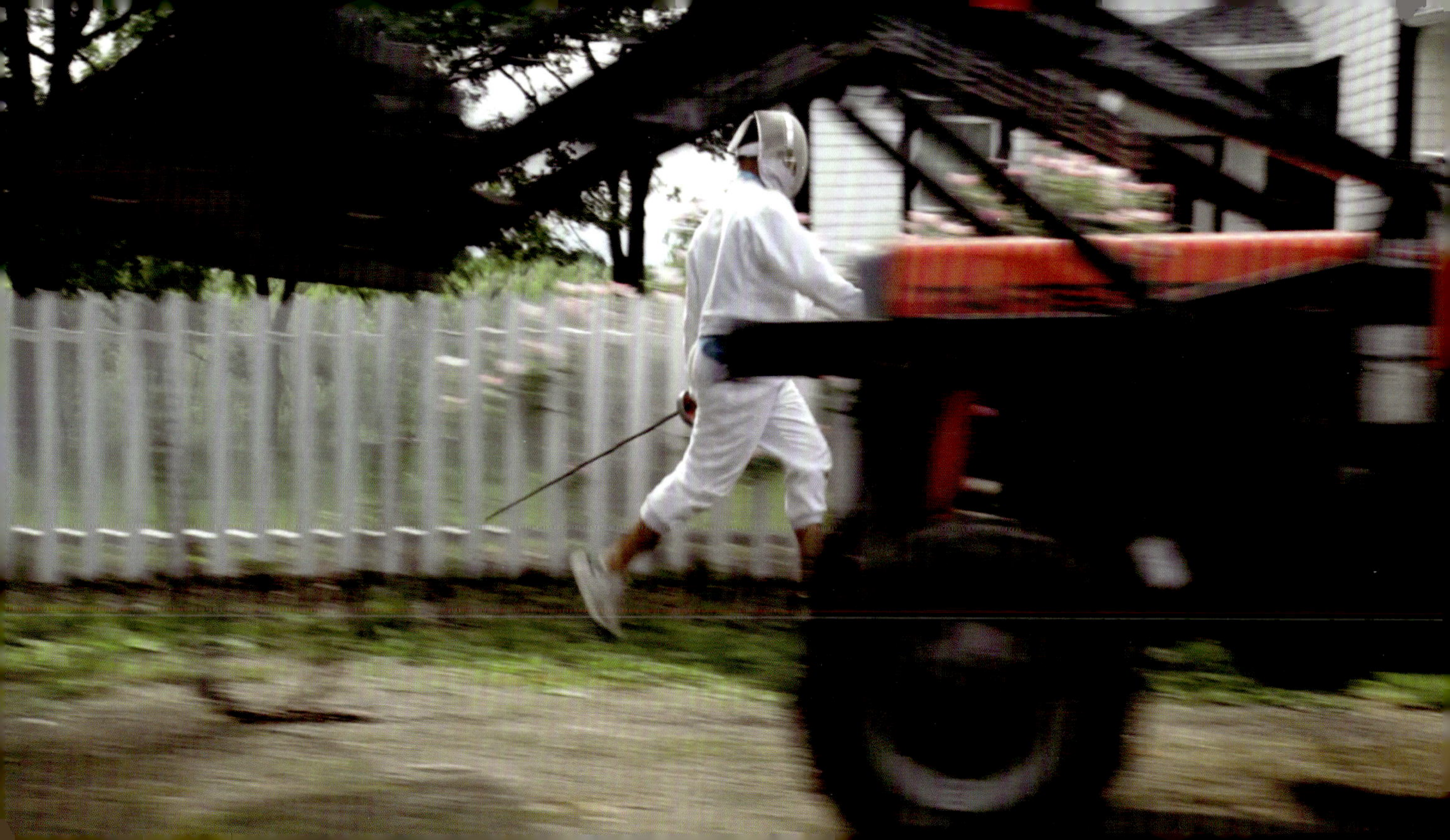

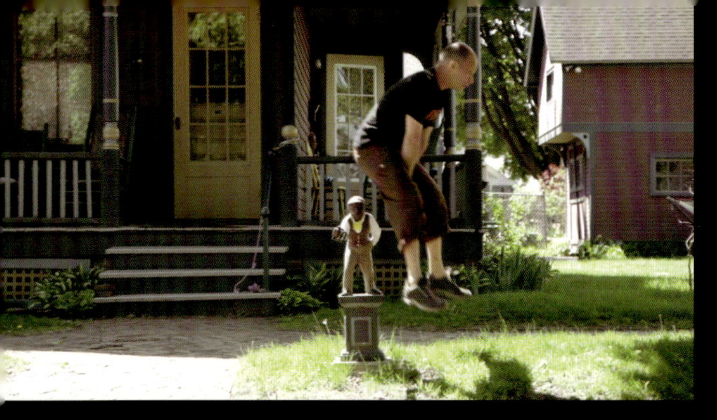
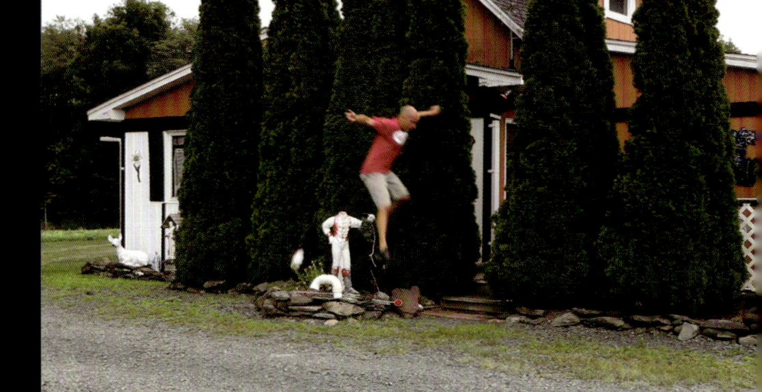
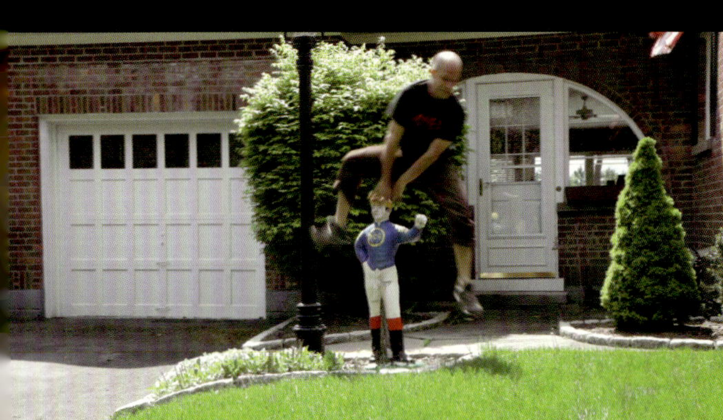
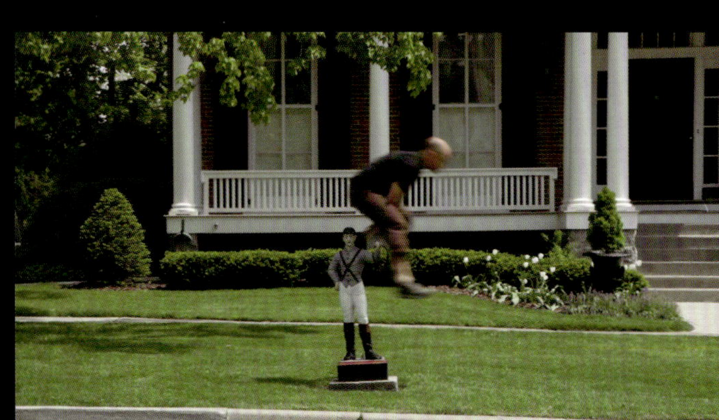

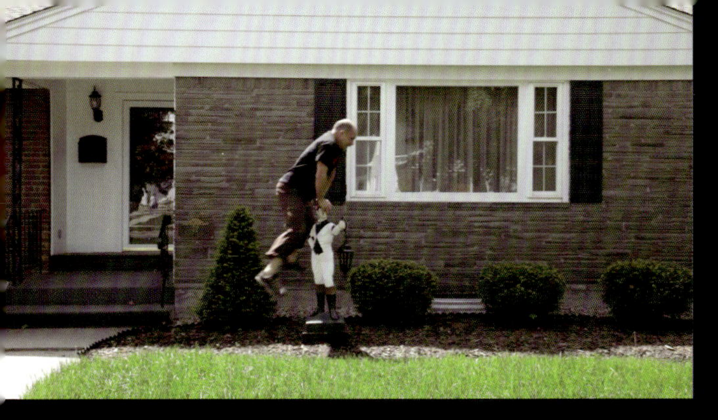
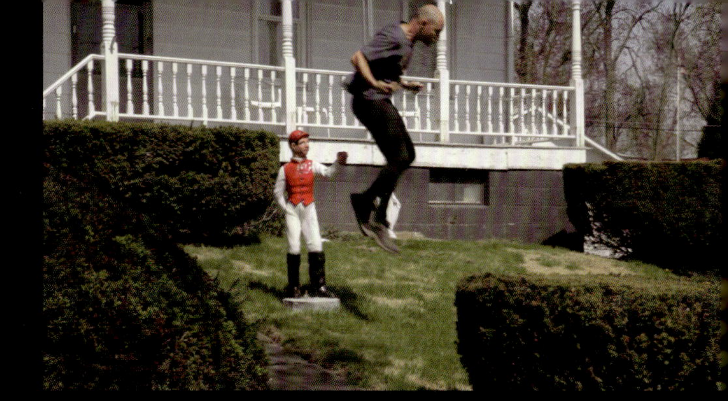
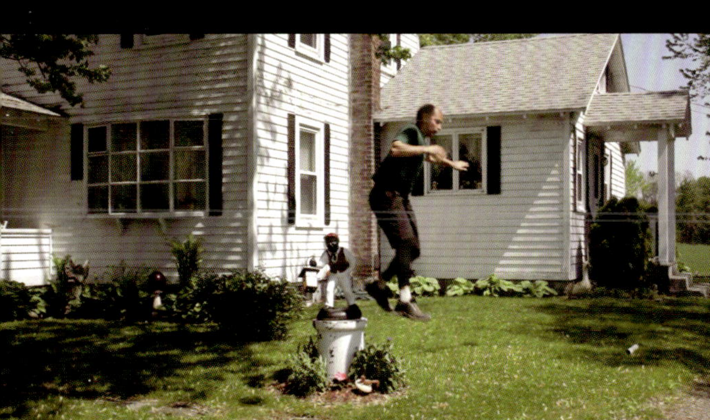
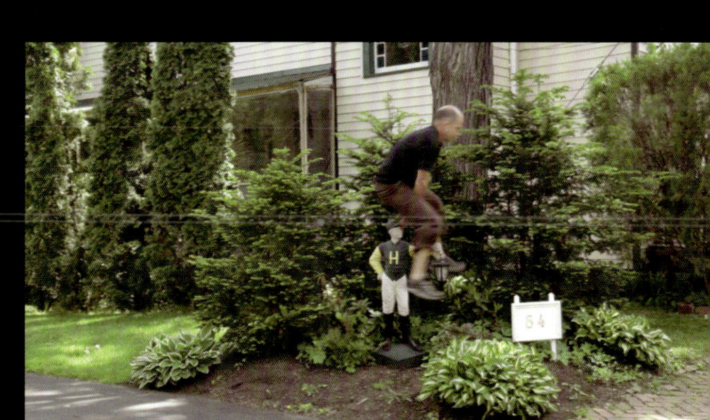

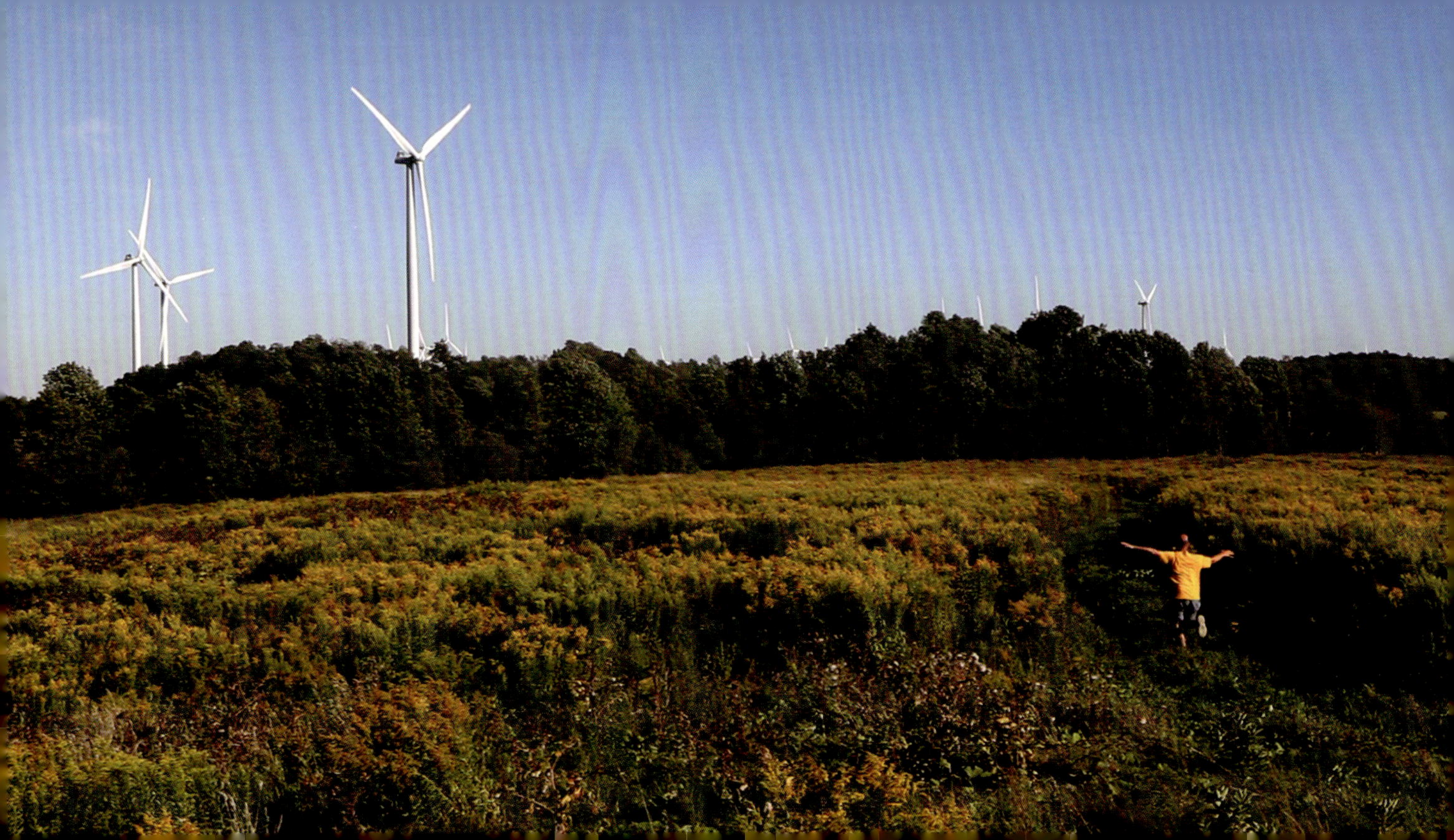

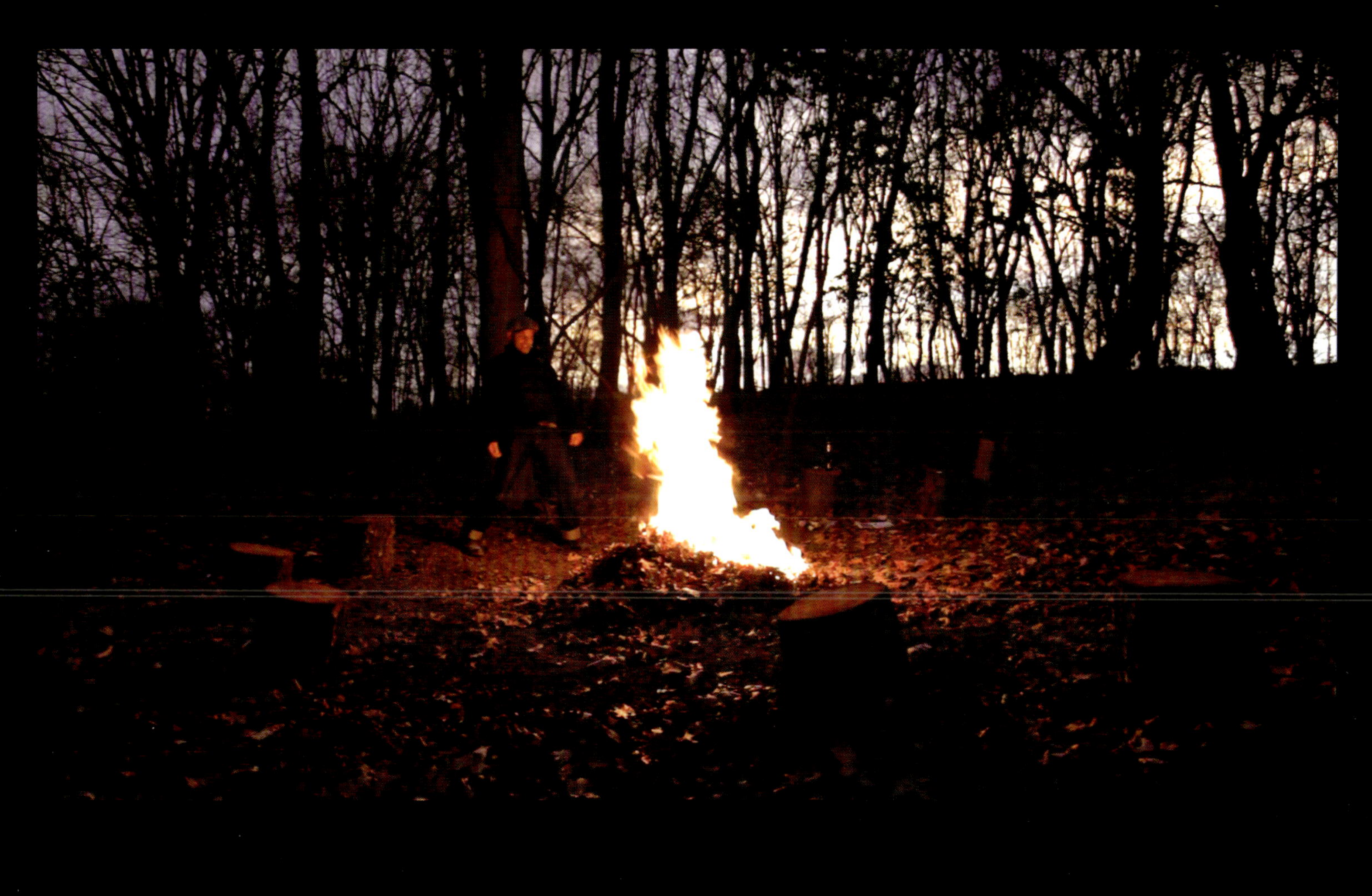

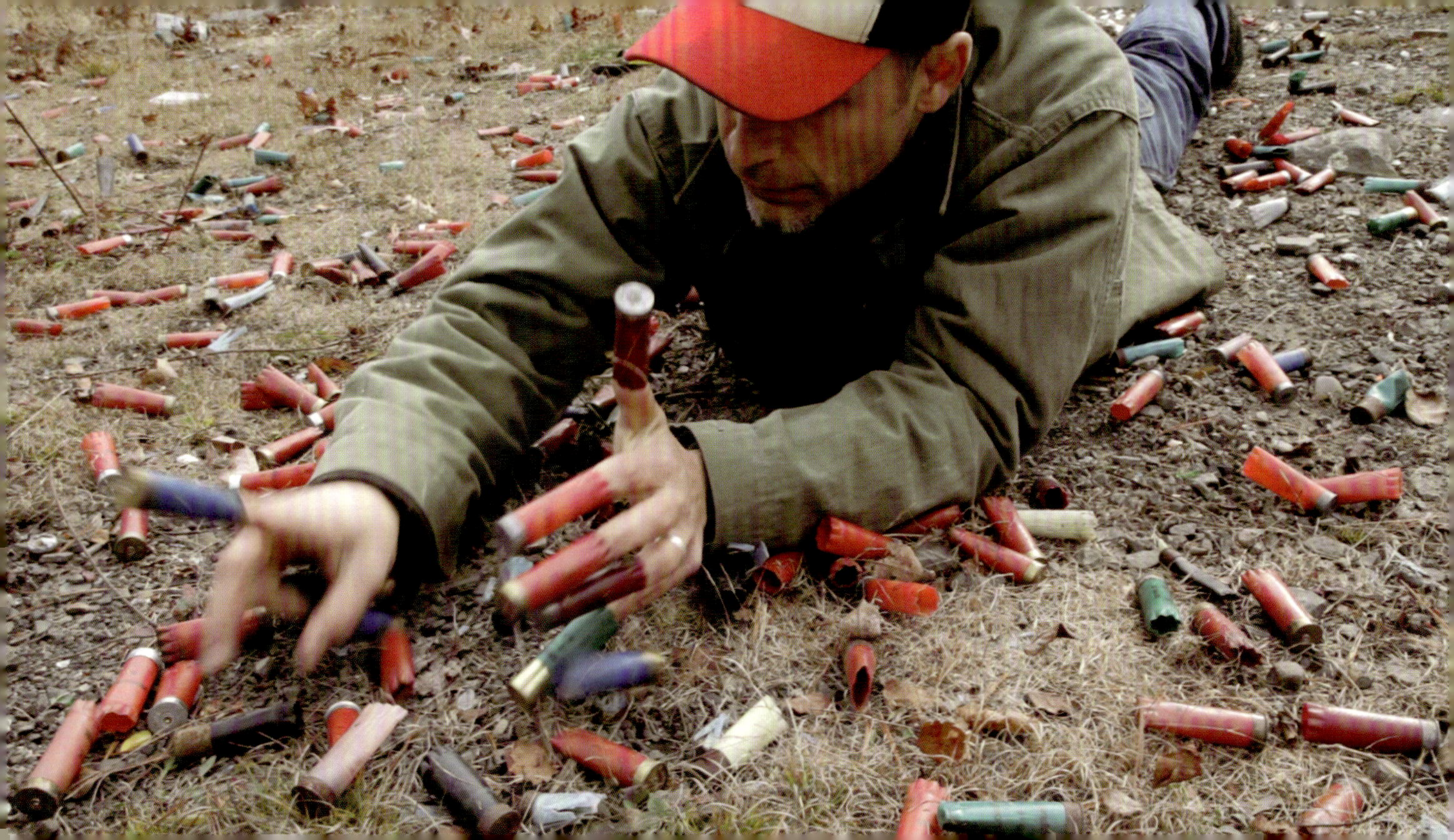

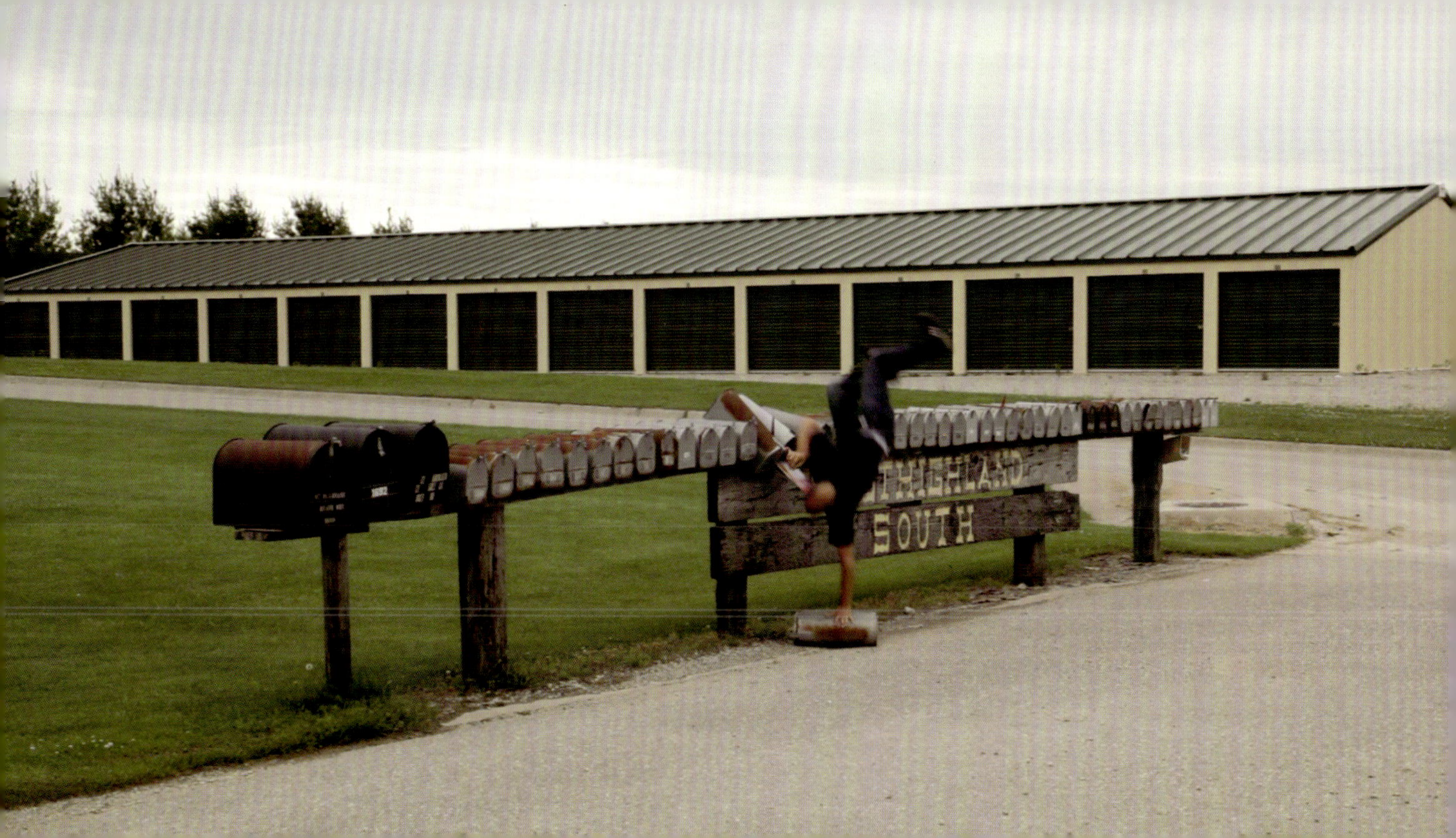

HIGHLAND
SOUTH

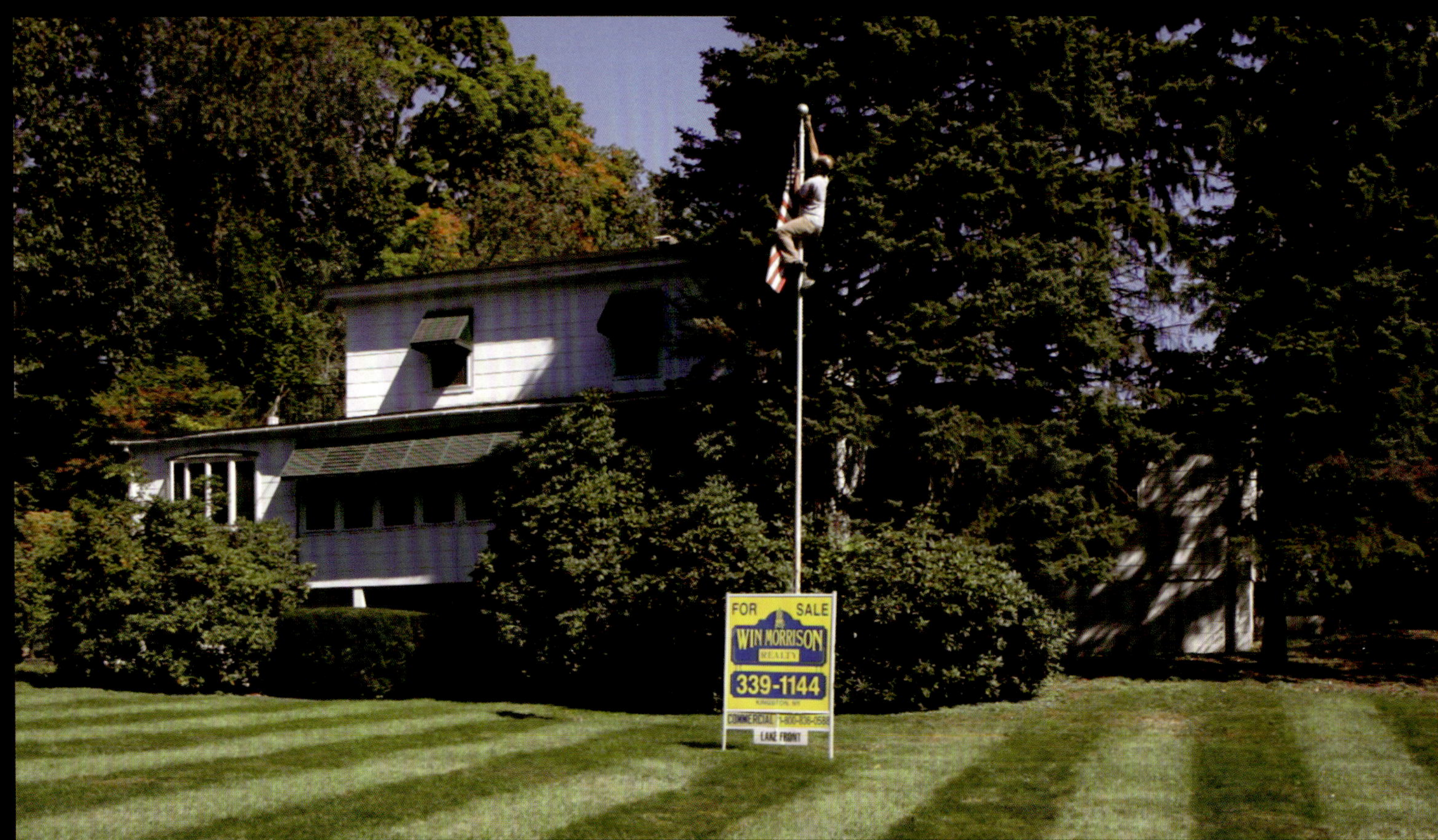

FOR SALE
WIN MORRISON
REALTY
339-1144
KINGSTON, NY
COMMERCIAL 1-800-836-0588
LAKE FRONT

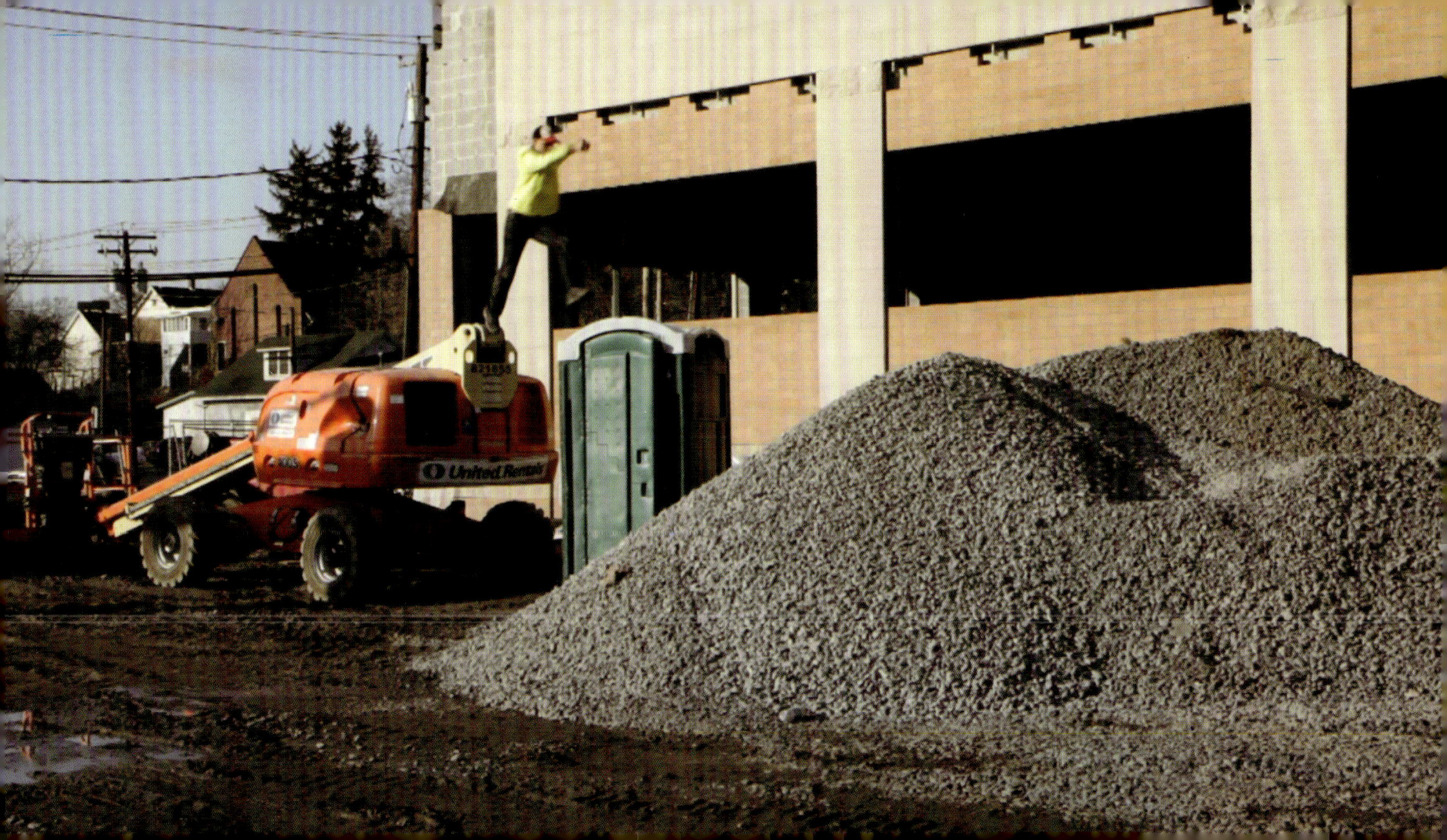

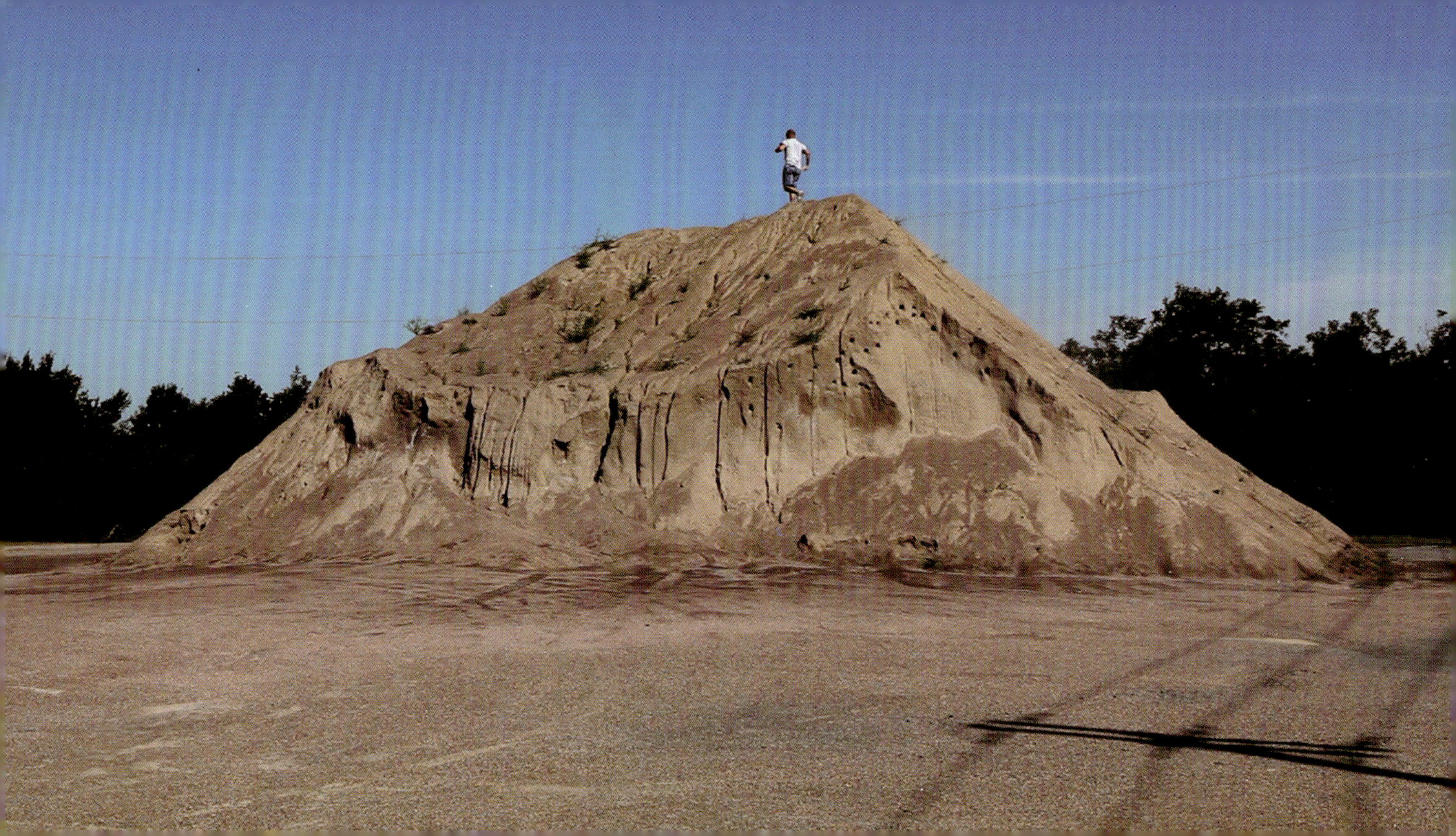

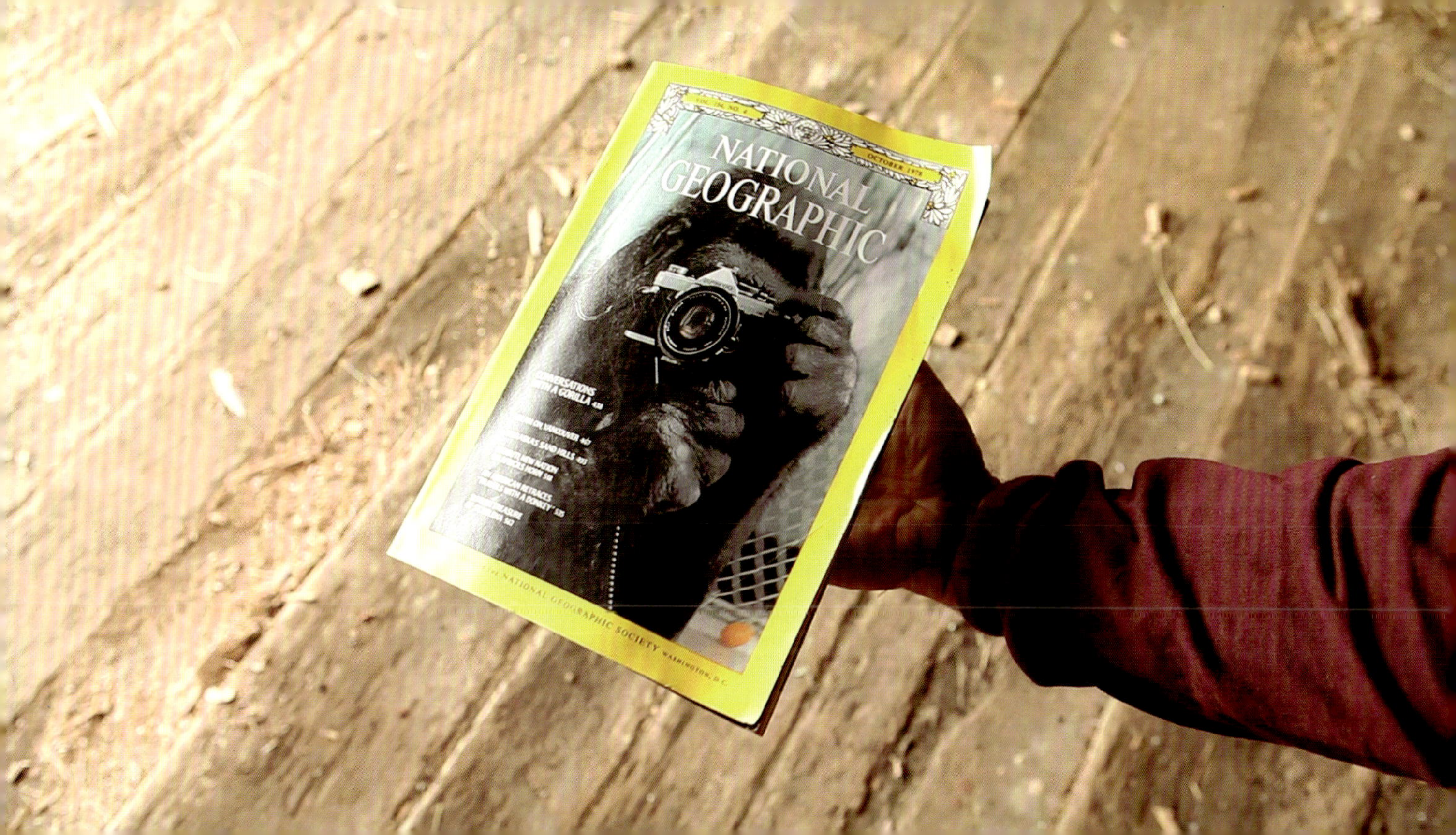

VOL. 154, NO. 4
OCTOBER 1978
NATIONAL
GEOGRAPHIC
CONVERSATIONS
WITH A GORILLA
NATIONAL GEOGRAPHIC SOCIETY WASHINGTON, D.C.

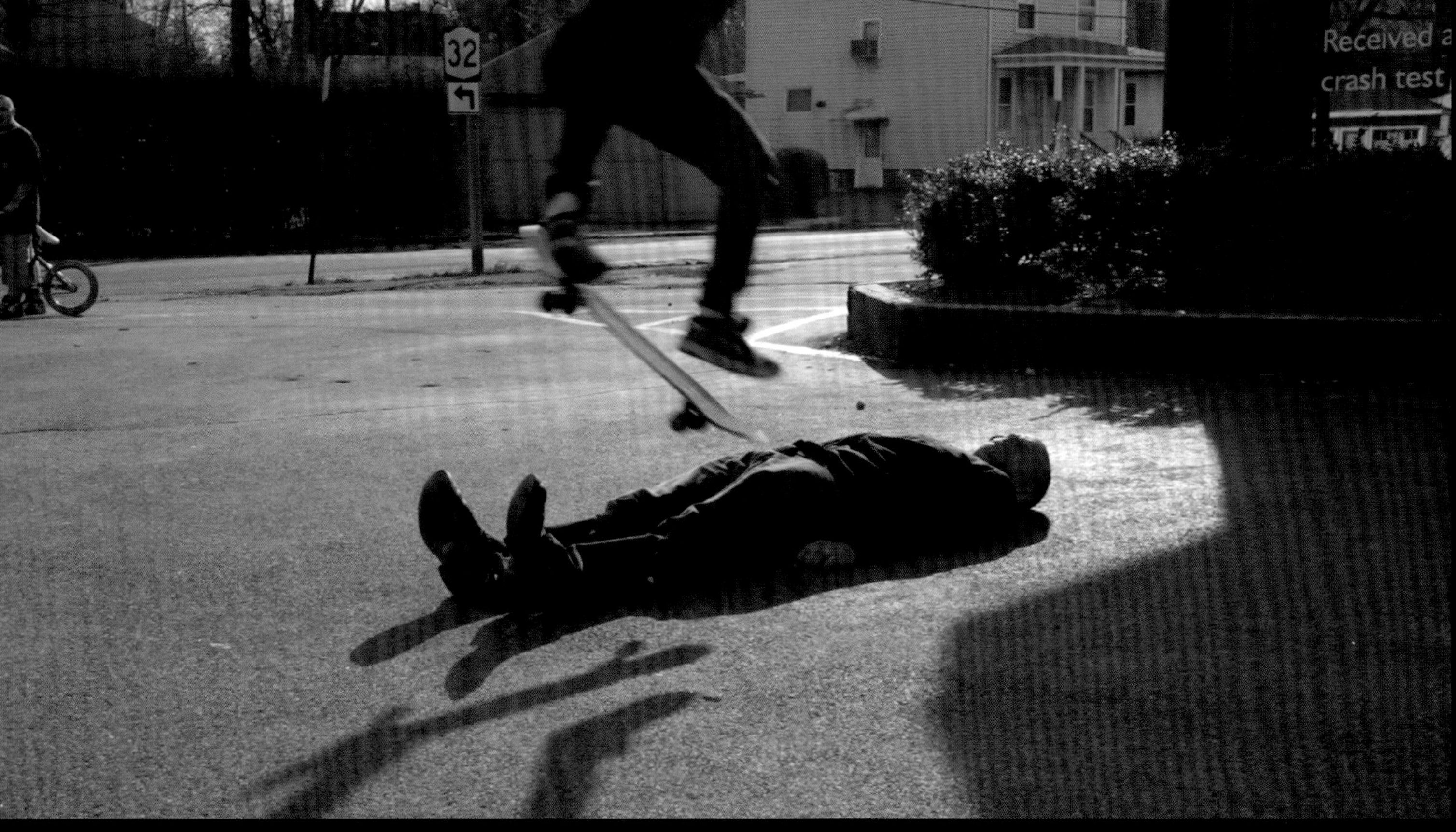

32
Received a
crash test

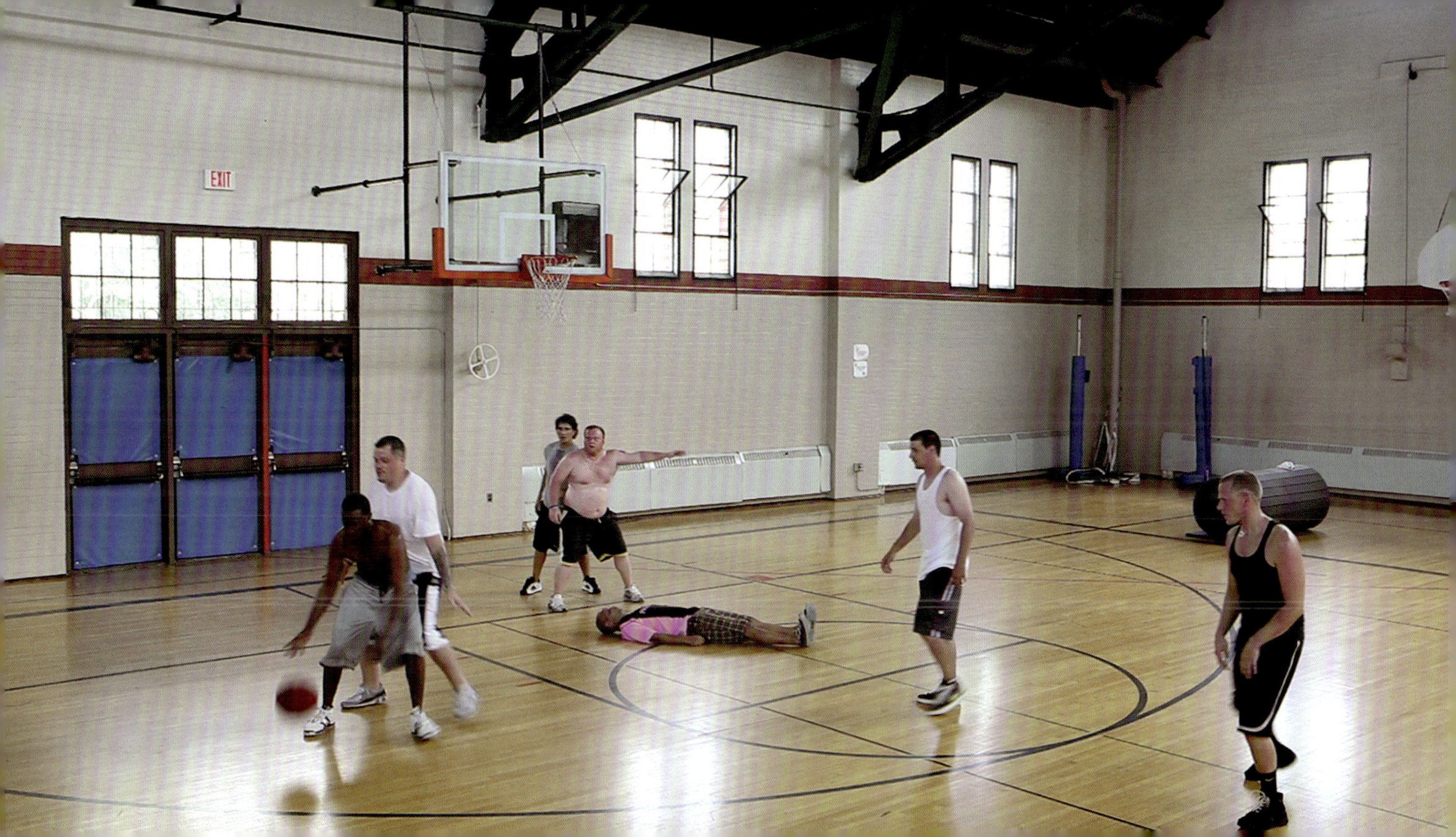

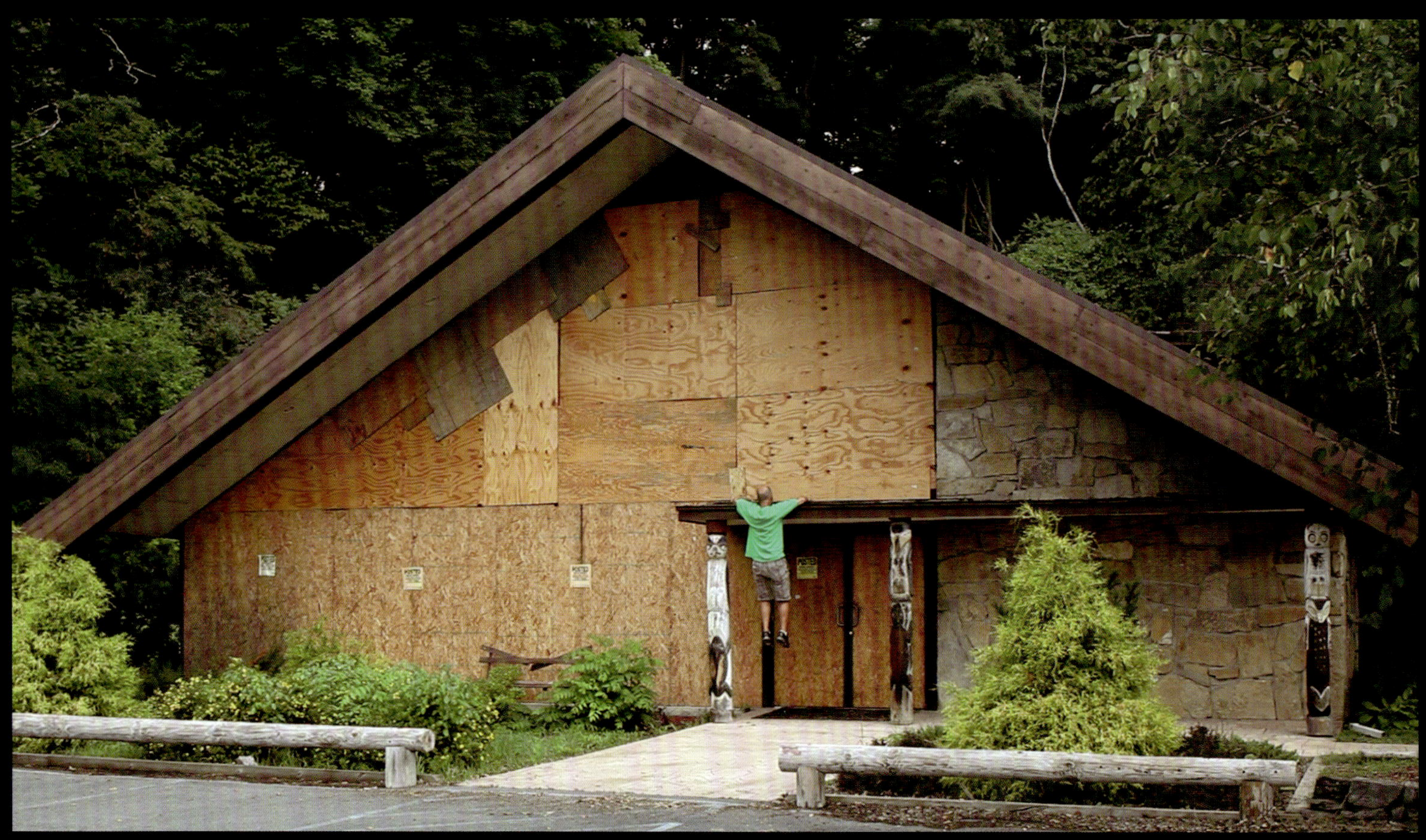

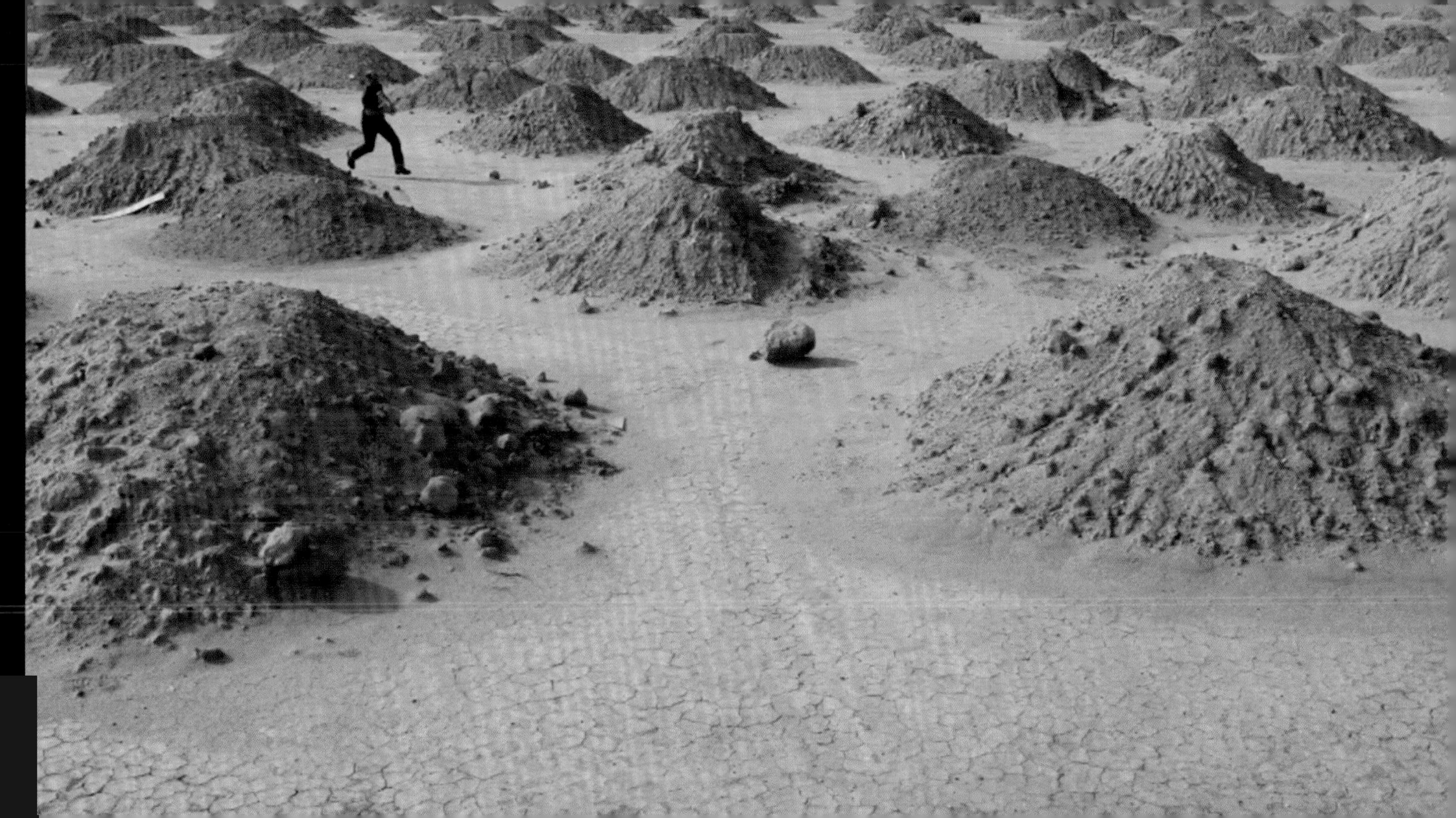

ARTIST

Malawi-born Tim Davis, a graduate of Bard College and Yale University, and a recipient of the Rome Prize from the American Academy in 2007, is an artist and poet who teaches at Bard College and is represented by the Greenberg Van Doren Gallery. Davis' recent solo exhibitions include *The New Antiquity*, Greenberg Van Doren Gallery, New York, *Kings of Cyan*, Mitterand + Sanz, Zurich, Switzerland, and *My Life in Politics* and *Permanent Collection* (both travelling). Along with a three-person exhibition at the Frances Lehman Loeb Center, Vassar College, Davis's work has been included in group exhibitions at Th-Inside, Berlin, Germany, American Academy in Rome, Italy, Tate Modern, London, England, Yancey Richardson Gallery, New York, P.S.1, Queens, New York, Museum of Modern Art, New York, White Cube, London, England, and many other venues. Davis's work is in the collection of numerous New York institutions, including the Dorsky Museum at SUNY New Paltz, the Metropolitan Museum of Art, the Museum of Modern Art, the Solomon R. Guggenheim Museum, the Whitney Museum of American Art, the Brooklyn Museum of Art, the Frances Lehman Loeb Art Center, Vassar College, and the Hirshhorn Museum, Washington D.C., the Norton Museum of Art, Palm Beach, Florida, the Milwaukee Art Museum, Wisconsin, and the Walker Art Center, Minneapolis, Minnesota.

CONTRIBUTORS

Thomas Bartscherer, Ph.D., is Assistant Professor of Humanities in Literature at Bard College and Director of Bard's Language and Thinking Program. Bartscherer's research and writings focus on tragic drama, aesthetics, and performance in the ancient Greek and modern German traditions; he also writes on technology, new media, and contemporary art. Bartscherer is co-editor of *Erotikon: Essays on Eros, Ancient and Modern* (University of Chicago Press, 2005) with Shadi Bartsch and *Switching Codes* (University of Chicago Press, forthcoming) with Roderick Coover.

Austin Kelley, Ph.D., Lecturer, Faculty of Arts & Sciences at New York University, is an author, the founding editor of *Modern Spectator*, and a contributing writer to the *New York Times*, the *New Yorker*, the *Wall Street Journal*, and *Men's Vogue*. In his writings, Kelley often analyzes the spaces and cultures of leisure (activities including reading, sport, and tourism) from literary, anthropological, and historical perspectives. He is currently working on a book about the cultural politics of the Olympics.

Brian Wallace, M.A., is curator at the Dorsky Museum at SUNY New Paltz. Since his appointment in 2006, he has organized exhibitions and artist projects including *Marco Maggi: New and Recent Works*; *Carrying: Pistol Packin' Pupils*; *Carolee Schneemann: Within and Beyond the Premises*; *analog catalog: Investigating the Permanent Collection*; *Habitats for Artists*; *Intimacies of Distant War*; *Panorama of the Hudson River: Greg Miller*; *Grace Bakst Wapner: A Scholar's Garden*; *Hudson Valley Artists 2007: The Uncanny Valley*; *Interpreting Utopia*; and *Judy Pfaff: New Prints and Drawings* and *Judy Pfaff Selects from the SDMA Collection*.